T0364363

Written
by
Markus Breitschmid

PARK BOOKS

Non-
Referential
Architecture

**Ideated
by
Valerio Olgiati**

The book *Non-Referential Architecture* has been in the making for some time. The two authors—the architect Valerio Olgiati and the architectural theoretician Markus Breitschmid—have known each other since 2005 and have had many conversations in Switzerland, the United States of America, and Portugal. The fruits of these conversations have been presented in several previous publications that took the form of books, essays, and interviews. The idea of compiling the present book arose in 2013. Its contents coalesced during multiple extended conclaves held in the Swiss Alps and in Alentejo. The book was ultimately written in Virginia.

Contents

Preface

This book is addressed to the makers of architecture, practicing architects as it were, and everyone else who is creatively invested in our built environment, such as urban planners and landscape architects. The book aims for two things: first, it is a tract that presents for architects a new way of seeing and comprehending the societal currents of the non-referential world within which they must operate by necessity; and, second, it is a pamphlet that intends to provide guidance and orientation on non-referential architecture. In other and more direct words: the book is the first step in a new framework for seeing the contemporary non-referential world as it presents itself to us as architects, and it offers architects a foundation for conceiving a non-referential architecture in that non-referential world.

Not unlike philosophers and other people who participate in forming our world, it is legitimate for us as architects to propagate a thesis. However, architects are not philosophers and they often lack the systematic approach of philosophers. On the other hand, architects have a quality that philosophers often lack: they are a bit like a sleuth, a kind of sniffer dog, capable of coalescing loose and disconnected occurrences creatively into an early and sometimes not fully matured embodiment of a new framework with a view to understanding something new that is in itself not yet fully matured. The famed historian Oswald Spengler admired architects for exactly that capability and suggested that when architecture is attempting to embody a cultural phenomenon, buildings "come early" while philosophy "comes late." As far as our own intention with this book goes, as architects we want to harvest the strength of that aesthetic "sleuthing" at our disposal. We aim to coalesce in a written form observations that we have made in the direction of a non-referential architecture.

It is important to make another distinction. This distinction relates to the many contributors who make up the discipline of architecture: it is the distinction between the creative maker of architecture, the practicing architect as such, on the one hand, and the interpreter, the critic, and the historian, on the other hand—the former builds, the latter evaluates. This is a book foremost for those who build. As such, the book supports the artistic making and the creative process and it is consciously written with that primary readership in mind, both in regard to how the subject matter is discussed and presented and the way it is structured and organized. Keeping this approach in mind, the book refrains from appearing too scholarly and including everything that scholarly academic texts typically contain. We consciously decided that, ideally, the examination in hand would mention no names, although we were aware of the difficulties that might pose. Hence the few names that have been referred to are only included when it seemed absolutely necessary for the orientation of the reader. Moreover, we decided to have no citations and to exclude the use of photographs, illustrations, and drawings—with one exception. We chose to omit illustrations so that our thesis of a non-referential architecture will not be interpreted as a stylistic recipe. Instead, it allows for the emergence of multiple formal possibilities in the mind of the reader. We ask the reader to imagine what a non-referential architecture should be like. In addition—despite the difficulty it posed for us as authors—we attempted to clarify our argument in the most general manner and largely without examples and counter-examples. We did so for the same reason justifying the absence of illustrations. Exceptions to this self-imposed measure also arose, mainly when we realized that the content is intangible without examples. Therefore, we aim to make our points not through comparisons of what exists but by means of self-evident arguments (it would be too lofty to call them philosophical propositions, but perhaps we can call them analytical-theoretical attempts). We consciously adopted this particular approach with the legibility of the text in mind: the thesis should be accessible for the reader with ease and obviousness. While consciously liberating itself from technical constraints of scholarship, this book also grants itself the liberty of making broad coalescing statements. Then again, our way of presenting our thoughts is neither entirely discouraged nor novel. With this approach, we take a cue from Friedrich Nietzsche, who offers multiple aphorisms in support of a departure from academic scholarliness and suggests that such liberties would present only seemingly "unfavorable conditions" if compared with more obdurate methods of erudition. Therefore, this liberation from academic texts does not imply that the book is not the product of intellectual work and the result of observation, analysis and synthesis, and reasoned speculation. Rather, and most importantly, as Nietzsche suggests, it is through such liberation that the book's "feet are winged." Every reader will easily identify that this book, and what is stated therein, is not devoid of ideational forefathers. Naturally, and without any intention of concealing such primogenitors, the book and its authors are indebted to those who have influenced, and thus helped to formulate, the thesis that is propagated here.

One other important delineation ought to be made. It is a limitation. This book on non-referential architecture is not an attempt to solve what might be perceived as "larger societal problems." Despite the fact that it does consider the fundamental currents of the contemporary non-referential world in very broad terms, the book does not do this. It does consider the world broadly but only with a view to demonstrating why non-referential architecture is the only possible way to make architecture today. However, the book does not alter or idealize any larger societal currents in any one direction. As a matter of fact, it very deliberately does not attempt to do so, as it embraces the world as it is and goes from there. We do not see ourselves as *Weltverbesserer,* "starry-eyed idealists" and "do-gooders," nor do we think that this is a chief task of architects.

This book aims to be as non-ideological as possible and strives to discuss architecture in our non-referential world as it currently happens to be—for good or bad.

Another limitation of the book stems from the fact that the authors conceived it as a tract that can be read in one or maybe two evenings, as many of us architects tend to be slow readers. We thought that "100 pages or so" should be sufficient to lay out what is on our minds. The desired brevity means that not every subject that is touched on is dealt with conclusively. The intention was to write and present a succinct book that introduces a new framework for conceiving architecture in a non-referential world. At times, this succinctness can only lead to a sprinkling of ideas, but with the understanding and acknowledgment that the strewn seeds will grow in the minds and hands of architects.

If architects are the primary future bearers of a non-referential architecture, it should also be stated in this preface that the thesis of a non-referential architecture implies a future-oriented image of the architect. The image of the architect as "author," in the sense of the individual who conceives and creates buildings, is not antiquated, as too many critics and educators like to suggest to young minds in the halls of academia. The model of the architect presented here, that is someone who operates successfully in our non-referential world, is timely and forward-striving, inasmuch as this architect is presented as a mentor and mastermind of a team with the propensity to be a creative figure and thinker, who is capable of building in a non-referential world.

Hence this book is an encompassing text for practicing architects aimed at helping them in their search for a foundational and principled professional position within the discipline of architecture—an intellectual apparatus so to speak—from which they can operate as architects who build in a non-referential world. This is the world that has grown radically different from the tenets of modernity and postmodernity that still largely occupy the institutional vessels of our profession. Architects reading this book may be inspired by the totality of the text, but it is also possible that they will only find stimulation and encouragement in one chapter or one principle defined in this book, so that they can then weave a new non-referential architecture in their own terms.

Valerio Olgiati
Markus Breitschmid

Introduction to Non-Referential Architecture

Non-Referential Architecture

We live in a non-referential world. Therefore, architecture must be non-referential. Non-referentiality is the only way to conceive buildings that make sense in a world in which simple attributions of meaning no longer exist. While it is unquestioned that architecture always possesses some social task, buildings can no longer be derived from a common social ideal, at least not in a direct way, because no such common social ideals as we might have shared in the past have endured in today's world. Non-referential architecture is not an architecture that subsists as a referential vessel or as a symbol of something outside itself. Non-referential buildings are entities that are themselves meaningful and sense-making and, as such, no less the embodiment of society than buildings were in the past when they were the bearers of common social ideals.

The widespread affective response of overcoming this apparent loss of content by means of imbuing buildings with meaning from extra-architectural sources is futile. In our non-referential world, architecture goes astray if the enrichment of buildings is to be sought by means of recourse to the extra-architectural. This misunderstood multidisciplinarity or transdisciplinarity is of no benefit to architecture itself—nor is it beneficial to architecture's social responsibility. Therefore, non-referential architecture is not "multicultural" architecture. However, it is impossible for architecture to be devoid of meaning; it cannot be an object of nothingness. Contrary to these widespread and prevalent extra-architectural attempts to enrich the buildings of today, architecture is first and foremost the conception, construction, and building of rooms; it deals with scenography and movements through rooms. As such, architecture engenders, above all else, a basic physical and sensual experience prior to also initiating intellectual interpretation. First and foremost, rooms trigger both an experience of space as well as a common human yearning to make sense out of that basic experience. That experience of space is basic and fundamentally architectonic. It is important to know that no discipline other than architecture itself has the ability to contribute anything of consequence to these fundamental architectonic conditions. If it engages anything at all, the extra-architectural tends to only engage the intellectual as it simply stands outside of what the art-form of architecture can convey. Instead of valuing buildings as a symbol of something that is based outside of the architectural—as was possible when common ideals existed and were widely acknowledged and understood by people—today, non-referential architecture has no other choice than to be purely architectonic. Non-referential architecture has no other choice because, for the first time in history, our society functions quite well without a fundamental comprehension of cultural and historical relationships.

The fact that no such fundamental comprehension of cultural and historical relationships exists, yet the world does not seem to be worse than before, is a momentous occasion in our understanding of how our world is supposed to function. This is new to all of us! This situation of a non-referential world affects architecture greatly: it is only as a purely architectonic object—and we do not refer here to an unrelated solitaire because an architectonic object can be everything from a fragment of a building to an entire city—that a building has the capacity to cause repercussions in the soul and mind of a person living in today's non-referential world.

The non-referential world is the world that demands each person to constantly align themselves with the world anew, since no fixed meanings can persist any longer. It is only predictable that philosophers also expanded the notion of the artist to men. The expanded notion of the artistic describes people as creatively equipped beings with the ability to form the totality of life-contexts, not unlike a work of art. As such, every person can be an architect of life. In our non-referential world, we all should build a world. Moreover, what is fundamentally different from the past is that now people do not build *one* world, but it is proposed that we all build *our* world. What is important for us architects is that the philosophical building of a world goes hand-in-hand with the literal act of building by actual architects. Instead of taking recourse to the extra-architectural to imbue buildings with sense, buildings themselves can be sense-making. As such, they can be fundamental in the social task of ordering a world.

The attempt to go outside of architecture to imbue buildings with added value is futile and belittles the capacity of architecture. To attempt to enrich buildings with more diverse facets is the old model of postmodern architecture, one that aimed for a so-called multicultural world. However, we are not living in the multicultural ideal of postmodernity any longer. We live in a non-referential world that is not governed by ever-increasing multitudes with the aim of somehow living in a balanced-out society in which all these values coexist. If it has not already ceased to exist, that model of society, namely the orderly coexistence of values, is rapidly dying. The multicultural world proposed the coexistence of affirmed sets of values. Its biggest challenge was to establish common and coherent notions of value in a society characterized by the diversity of people from around the world. The key concept behind such attempts is integration. This concept is subject to a postmodernist ideology of the 1960s to 1980s, namely one that assumes societal aims to be relatively homogenous, one that presumes very similar needs and interests. Today, this is no longer the case. Today, not only are there very few people who would even know what these needs, interests, and values would be, these values certainly do not carry with them the strength of a widespread consensus so as to give structure and order to our world. In today's non-referential world, societal aims are differentiated into a plethora of individuals and groups with completely different interests that make coalescence all but impossible. The image of the sociological population structure shows that common identifiable needs of people do not exist, because even the notion of a more or less coherent "people" no longer exists. In the non-referential world, we do not share a "project" or a "program" any longer, as we did fervently in the epoch of modernity and, critically, in postmodernity. Scholars have labeled this encompassing circumstance of our world an alarmist "world-conceptual emptiness." We, instead, would like to describe the currents of our non-referential world less feverishly and less vehemently as a *realism without an interpretation.*

These larger currents of the world do interest us. As architects, however, we have to recognize that non-architects do not know the actual cause of architecture. Sometimes this not-knowing the cause of architecture also applies to architects. Therefore, we can also include architects among the culprits who mistakenly believe that the salvation of architecture in our disorienting times lies in architectural approaches that take the economic, the ecological, and the political as the chief bases for making architecture. They do so with the hope of imbuing it with relevance and moral righteousness. Equally misguided is the approach of architects who understand building as an overtly artistic endeavor by means of permeation with esoteric-rhetoric concepts, when, in fact, these conceptualizations are mostly a deaden thing devoid of life. In both of these misguided approaches, architecture relies on something that is outside the realm of the architectonic. If such architects talk about architecture, they do so only through aspects of their own specifically non-architectonic viewpoints and also base their judgments on criteria taken from these non-architectonic approaches. Yes, it is a fact that architecture is also affected by mathematics, sociology, biology, ethics, and art—to list just a few—but, ultimately, these disciplines and their specific viewpoints for judgment cannot contribute to the actual thing at the fore, namely, the task of projecting buildings—by which is meant the mind-generative act of conceiving, the "throwing forth" of buildings (and better describes what architects actually do than the commonly used term "designing"). To state it here, not for the last time: a building, for and by itself, has the innate capability not only of being purely architectonic, it can also be sense-making. In that respect, non-referential architecture relies on and is justified by the basis of the most fundamental quality and characteristic of what a building can be, namely, it is its own sense-making thing. The philosopher Martin Heidegger once said in reference to this: "The building is in the stone."

Non-referential architecture liberates architecture from the vessel of non-architectural meanings so that it can make sense for the people of the twenty-first century who do not live alongside fixated ideals embedded in those meanings. Yet to define architecture as its own discipline is not new. However, what is new is the increasing heterogeneity of our society. It is not pessimism to determine that we live in a world where increasingly fewer guidelines and rules exist that are common to most of us. Today, institutions no longer exist that possess the strength to put together or even just hold together our society—as the church or state did in the past. The church increasingly relinquished its coalescing power from the Enlightenment. The state, which followed the church as that uniting force, is now disintegrating in front of our eyes. Many of the most intelligent and knowledgeable people have come to the conclusion that this is a marked characteristic of our current age, namely that it is no longer possible to really believe in anything today—not only in a religious sense but equally in a political, artistic, or scientific sense. This does not mean that no great human achievements occur today. On the contrary! However, such achievements and innovations do not amount to an integration of some kind of coherent set of widely shared values; nor do they point in the direction of an institution that would help to order such an elusive set of conducts. We could say that we are living in an increasingly non-ideological world. We live in an epoch of all-encompassing disenchantment, in which the only enchantment is, perhaps, the common disenchantment. This situation should perhaps be lamented, but it does not help to do so. We do not lament it, actually, and non-referential architecture deals with this world, in which simple attributions of meanings no longer exist, as an opportunity to make a liberated architecture befitting a non-referential world.

For non-referential architecture, the following question arises: how can a building make sense? Less broadly: in our extremely unrelated, heterogeneous, polyvalent, unconventional, informal, decentralized, and spread-out world, which is increasingly freed of ideologies, how can we design, or again, project buildings that possess a general validity and common value beyond the particular meaning they might have for one private individual?

That non-referential architecture does not represent a particular style of architecture for buildings and cities or any other kind of ideology—various styles or ideologies for conceiving buildings and planning cities which an architect, a client, a city planner, a politician can turn to or not—is evident from a view of architectural theory of the last half-century that emerged since Robert Venturi presented his landmark treatise *Complexity and Contradiction in Architecture.* Almost hand in hand with Venturi's influence on architecture, we must also not subscribe to Aldo Rossi's equally old dictum of the "autonomy of architecture" in order to accept that, at present, architecture may only be derived from itself. Even architectural thinkers at a considerable remove from Venturi and Rossi point in the same direction: Peter Eisenman calls for the complete substitution of semantics with syntax, Bernard Tschumi sees no fixed relationship between architectural form and events, Peter Zumthor seeks an architecture of "civilizing innocence," Jacques Herzog and Pierre de Meuron are advocates of "specific form," in which architecture represents nothing, and Rem Koolhaas exempts the interrelationship of the meaning of buildings from the identity and shape of buildings and introduced his notion of the technology-alike "generic." Each of these examples represents attempts at the liberation of architecture from the extra-architectural. We are witnesses of a movement towards a pure architecture—in other words, of a growing tradition towards a liberated architecture that is no longer ideological, or more broadly stated, is no longer symbolic and reliant on images. However, all of these attempts by the above-listed architects are still indebted to modernism, inasmuch as they are, in fact, born out of a reaction to modernism—sometimes articulated against modernism and sometimes as an extension of modernism. They all astutely and keenly realized the emergence of a heterogeneous and polyvalent world and they proposed how architecture could react to it. However, none of them embraced the polyvalent world affirmatively. In all of their various approaches, these architects assigned the viewer of their buildings the position of a "recipient" and a kind of a more or less directly or indirectly involved "spectator." With Eisenman and Tschumi this recipient is asked to deconstruct their world in an intellectual exercise; with Herzog & de Meuron and Zumthor the recipient must undergo a ritualized cleansing to reach either monk-like or Buddhist-like private contemplative innocence; and with Koolhaas, the visitor is a spectator who accepts the scientization, specialism, and fragmentation of the self. Nevertheless, all of these were important steps towards where architecture is today and each of them has indelibly prepared the ground for a non-referential architecture.

The thesis of "non-referential architecture" not only radicalizes these attempts at liberation, it turns the page from the architecture of postmodernism and late-modernism of 1960 to 2000—which, it must be reiterated, is ultimately still very much embedded in the tenets of earlier modernism and moves forward toward a non-referential architecture that has largely left behind or has absorbed the conceptions of the "Modern Project." The "Modern Project" is referred to as a substantially political movement that posits the human mind as the origin of all things. Its chief concepts are individualism, liberalism, Marxism, mechanism, rationalism, scientism, secularism, subjectivism, and relativism. The fact that we have left the "Modern Project" of modern and postmodern architecture behind and have entered something new has also been realized, somewhat reluctantly, by Rem Koolhaas. In a lecture presented at Harvard University in 2016, he stated that "people over fifty have a tendency to worry, and people under fifty have a tendency not to care." What is detected here is not so much that people today do not care but they have figured out how not to be seduced by 20th-century notions such as "project" and "program." Today, people want to confront the complexities of life in a non-ideological way that does not embrace significance referentially. Modernism and postmodernism, the former with optimism and the latter as a critique, were still able to convincingly believe in a consensus of value—a world that was ultimately still governed by a rather fixated moral code and values. No such certainties exist today. The postmodernist architectural discourse confronted the socio-political complexities of urban life but its proposals were aided by the accepted viability of the referential "Modern Project." The task of today's non-referential architecture is a different one: its buildings have to be significant in a world that does not embrace significance. It is a fundamental shift from an architecture that offers its inhabitants a way of participating in a life-affirming known totality they believe in, and move toward an architecture that offers inhabitants a way to build a life-assuring totality that they believe does ultimately not exist.

For the practicing architect, the following problem arises: how can a single building exist in only one singular, albeit a significant, way, without being derived from an ideological "superstructure" that no longer exists?

It must be concluded: in a world without fixed values and rules, as we find it today, the idea for one single building by the architect is the only thing that gives meaning to that building because the architect cannot rely on a consistent set of values that would be consistently shared by the people using the building. This new societal situation, however, does not mean that the architect should act in isolation. On the contrary: it is the task of the architect to understand the fundamental societal currents—as polyvalent as they might be—of their time so as to ultimately guide the intentions for their buildings. Architects are not becoming less important, as we hear more and more often; the opposite is, in fact, the case. Without institutional guidelines and without societal commonalities that may serve architectural orientation as we have known it in the past, it is now the architect's task to design buildings that mean something—not a fixed meaning or program, as in the old modern and postmodern days or in epochs even further back in time—but to design buildings that still carry a sense about something existential about a person's life. This situation describes the new and undeniably difficult state in which we find ourselves today. This situation is new and challenging but it is as the world presents itself today. Any attempt to resuscitate old societal models is futile.

Today's architecture must be non-referential. There is no other option because any attempt to ideologically idealize and fixate it into some sort of a "school of thought" almost immediately renders it obsolete. However, non-referentiality does not mean that there is no standard for architecture today. There is no room for a jovial "anything goes," notwithstanding how serious that provocation was considered when it was perceptively issued half a century ago. Of chief importance for the architect who intends to design buildings today is the necessity to vacate the claim that has stewarded architecture for a long time, namely, that architecture is referential. Non-referential architecture must speak to the unbounded and non-ideological mental agility of people who live in that non-referential world of today. Therefore, a building cannot be historical or symbolical (both of these terms are used here in their broadest philosophical scope) in the sense that it represents something above and beyond itself, because no consensus exists as to what that above and beyond would possibly be. A building exists only for itself.

That a building exists only for itself is not at all problematic, as some might interject. It can be understood in a similar way to when traditional rationalist metaphysics was overcome by introducing aesthetics as a new philosophical discipline. Not unlike aesthetics as a then-new epistemological possibility, a building has the capacity by itself to encapsulate everything. Therefore, a building does not require external systems to justify itself in the same way that aesthetics could no longer be seen as a somehow inferior philosophical science compared to ethics and logic. It is possible that the physical presence of the building itself encompasses everything, including the highest and most eternal of mankind's shared wonderment.

Instead of attempting to embody ideals that no longer exist or do not possess the strength to coalesce, the purpose of a building is to encourage people to think and to enter into a discourse with that building and, by extension, with the world: a building, therefore, must be sense-making. However, sensemaking is not understood as meaning that a building is a receptacle of some external meaning applied to the building, but rather the building itself—because it is a fundamental constellation— helps its occupant to construct sense. The best buildings cause the kind of repercussions that architecture always brings forward: buildings bring forward a discourse between the "here" and the "there," between the "I" and the "unknown." Non-referential buildings trigger such discourses. Nevertheless: buildings represent nothing. Instead, buildings make sense by means of their presence. It is best to understand a building as an object that makes people creative.

Today, buildings are too often conceived as an expression of economic, ecological, and political concepts. No matter what extra-architectural impetus leads to a building, what such referential buildings all have in common is a loss of their ability to be general. In other words, while supposedly giving a building "depth" and meaning, extra-architectural content does the opposite. While a building conceived in that referential way might be interesting in that one particular way in which the architect conceived it, it tends to lack a general validity beyond the particular references made. Good examples of architecture with extra-architectural content are the many recent museums in which something is commemorated, often with ambitious historical references. However, we note—not only in those cases: the inclusion of extra-architectural themes arrests our imagining of how we conceive a building. It remains trapped in a specific theme and triggers little imagining with regard to architecture and the world at large. Such buildings suffocate in the referential.

Besides the more common recourse toward referentiality in architecture, as described above, there is one more problematic approach that must also be pointed out. Sometimes buildings are conceived in an overtly artistic approach. We could also call it a conceptual approach. This approach is often highly rhetorical. And it often appears esoteric. While this conceptual approach also recognizes that referentiality is untenable in our time, the "emptying" of buildings by means of radically conceptualizing them so that they carry no sense at all anymore is not desirable either. Yes, the "artistic" or "conceptual" approach is also very aware of the problem of referentiality. It also aims to free buildings from historical and symbolic connotations and images. However, the proposal of the "artistic" or "conceptual" approach is to clean the building of any kind of sense. The process with which it attempts to achieve this "emptying" involves the "found" and the "incidental." This cannot be the answer either because it propagates that the precise and well-conceived existence of architectonic order alone will engage human beings in a meaningful way. However, architectonic order for and by itself is not sense-making, even if it is established in an internally coherent way. This self-consciously "artistic" or "conceptual" approach (labeled as such because it seeks inspiration from conceptual art) is problematic because it tends to retreat to a private capsule in which one built idiosyncrasy stands next to the next built idiosyncrasy. Such an approach brings forward muteness because these buildings lack sense-making ideas.

It must be stressed and reiterated that, even if it is the most rigorous and coherent formulation, the establishment of an architectonic order alone is not sense-making but rather a mechanistic construct not unlike a perfectly engineered clockwork mechanism. There is a reason why people customarily do not count clockwork mechanisms as belonging to the truly aesthetic domain, their mechanical beauty notwithstanding.

Naturally, this raises the question as to how a sense-making architectural idea is brought to realization. What is it then exactly that gives a building its spatial and formal sense-making expression? Indeed, a kind of a basic precondition exists that cannot be avoided in buildings: the physical experience of space. Alberto Giacometti once said about his sculptures that the best thing about them is that one can touch them. We say that the best thing about buildings is that one can physically experience their rooms. Such experience of space is an undisputed, as it were, "raw" material with which any building must deal. It is the key to non-referential architecture.

In this respect, by means of their presence, rooms give buildings, subjective universality. The experience of space is present always and everywhere for everybody. This may read as too lapidary but it is certainly not so: the seemingly "simple" or "basic" room of a building already contains its representations in manifold ways. Rooms are for and by themselves significant. At the most basic, we can say that rooms make us experience the victory over matter. That victory over the matter of material is how a building becomes sense-making. It is a basic experience for all men and women. Understood in these terms, the form of rooms—both inside and outside—ultimately remains the most general architectonic of a building. It is form that brings to people an added cultural value and it is form that sets individuals and society in motion. Everything else, economy, ecology, history, politics, and all the other extra-architectural content, is not only not decisive but also narrowly referential. These aspects are not decisive because they are not generally valid for a building. Today, people hold no value-consensus about all of these extra-architectural importations, and it is a mistake to make buildings dependent on such non-general values. Precisely because it is unable to rely on any larger consensus, non-referential architecture can only be of general validity if it expresses something that is real and actual, as generally valid as possible, and as close as possible to be true, not unlike the most basic victory over the matter of material. Therefore, above all else, non-referential architecture is a question of form, namely, the conceiving of rooms on the outside and inside. Form causes an experience as space that is sense-making.

Our time is a fascinating time for architects; in no other previous age did architecture have to be as purely architectonic. Architects have to form rooms without extra-architectural references. In our non-referential world of the twenty-first century, the social conditions have developed in such a way that the doors are now open for buildings that stand for nothing else other than themselves—this is not intended, of course, in the sense of isolated objects in social isolation. Therefore, how an architect conceives their buildings with regard to form and the subsequent sense-making experience of space decides whether a building is significant or not. To clarify: even the magical and mystical are ultimately a part of that sense-making experience that the architect invents with their building. Architecture exists in the realm of the architectonic inasmuch as it does not need multidisciplinary alliances with extra-architectural domains, nor does it want to be the expression of an ordering system devoid of something sense-making for people. If a building is pure architecture, in that its architecture is derived from architecture, then it is entirely possible that a building can exist in only one and no other way and still be generally significant, even in a world that does not want to know about significance any longer.

After Postmodernity: Non-Referential World

We are living in a non-referential world that differs from the postmodernity of the last four decades of the twentieth century. Our society has undergone a second enlightenment in the past twenty years or so. However, this non-referential world is not yet widely accepted by the architectural community. The discipline of architecture still lingers in essentially old doctrines of modernist and postmodernist models to justify its work. Therefore, some explanation needs to be provided here to indicate the new societal streams on which non-referential architecture is based.

The key propagators and their key contributions have already been mentioned. We refer here again to Venturi's *Complexity and Contradiction in Architecture* because it is also a particularly good example of the argument that postmodernity is locked in the paradigms of the eighteenth-century Enlightenment, the same Enlightenment that also brought about the architectural modernism of the twentieth century. An important point in the context of our thesis is that modernity and postmodernity were epochs of a world that had ideals and believed in those ideals. Architecture was projected in reference to those ideals. As a consequence of that dependency, for example, it made perfect sense to call for one style or another, most famously the "International Style." As a matter of fact, despite the fact that—not unlike "history," the other distinctly modern and postmodern invention—modernity sometimes fought against such a label, the notion of "style" is a hallmark of modernity and postmodernity. It is important to realize this because, as has been pointed out previously, the non-referential world is not only no longer symbolical with regard to images of any kind, it is also no longer historical in its nature.

Society has gone through such fundamental upheavals that, today, it is not an overstatement to speak of a "second enlightenment" or a "new enlightenment." which confronts us in every aspect of our lives every single day.

When Venturi presented his *apologia* in 1966, he did so as a modern architect who was steeped in the tenets of modern architecture. It was almost impossible for Venturi, in his time, to conceive what it would mean to live and operate in a truly and thoroughly polyvalent world, one of the key terms of his treatise. From his modernist foundation of a monovalent world, Venturi did indeed demand a polyvalent world but he did not know what it was. Therefore, Venturi was thinking modernism through to its end. He was the interface that ended modernism and began postmodernism, yet the true paradigm shift was yet to occur. This is also why Venturi's call for a new framework for architecture has something subversive to it, that is when he aims for a compositional plurality and assemblages of cultural signage. He was the monovalent sleuth who detected the beginnings of a polyvalent world in architecture, but he did not yet foresee a polyvalent society, probably because it did not yet exist or because its full effects were not yet foreseeable. This is the reason why his plurality largely played itself out in the compositional realm of architecture. However, his subversive credo did push open the door for a deconstructive movement that would, indeed, follow. Today, there is nothing subversive about claiming that we live in a non-referential world. The non-referential world is the established world. Today, all of the subversive attempts of the 1960s to the 1980s have been absorbed and are accepted. However, it goes without saying that only a handful of architects have fully integrated this major philosophical and societal shift into their thinking.

The vast majority of the architectural profession, along with many theorists, critics, and historians, have not taken the step, of which Venturi had a vague idea when he propagated his theory 50 years ago. More often than not, architectural discourse still lingers in a modernist orthodoxy and in a codex that is half a century or more old. If you listen to how critics at architecture schools defend their arguments as to why certain projects lack this or that quality, you can observe how the tremendous changes that have occurred have scarcely entered the architectural discourse. If you consider the windmill-like propagation of credos by critics, you would be forgiven for having mistaken yourself to be still living in the political climate of 1968—with possibly one identifiable addition to the critiquing of projects, namely, the ubiquitous demand for context as the seemingly paramount moral value for architects and their buildings.

We live in a thoroughly heterogeneous, polyvalent, plural, decentralized, non-referential world in which everything is possible anywhere at any given point in time. What is fundamentally different to the conditions that prevailed as recently as two decades ago is the fact that today everybody—and we mean really everybody—knows about it. Our mobility and the way we communicate with each other and how we inform each other are merely the most obvious and most recognizable differences between now and twenty years ago. More significantly than the impact of these technological innovations, we do not seriously embrace any kind of firmament above us and solid ground underneath us today.

It is now a little more than a lifetime ago since broader philosophical discussions began to speak of a "transcendental homelessness" and a fundamental "disenchantment of the world." These discussions followed the earlier Nietzschean pronouncement which observed that people had "killed" the binding and meaningful firmament that had sheltered us from the brittleness of cold nature for a very long time. The modernist remedy for such laments was, of course, to place itself in a quasi-demonic allure in which productivity was elevated to the status of old-time religion, while at the same time the ever-increasing complexity of the world induced an end of naïve storytelling. The axiomatic summary of that program was the modernist "disenchantment of the world."

From our vantage point, all of this is part of our intellectual "mother's milk" as administered to us in school and at the university. And, indeed, such an interpretation of modernity still appears to serve as our diagnostic tool, including such terms as alienation and reification. This is also the ideological status quo that remains embedded in the academy. What its propagators have in common is that they want to be "critical" because they are convinced that the world somehow needs saving. A compilation that subsumed that ideological stance and gained much traction in the architectural discourse goes by the title of *The Anti-Aesthetic. Essays on Postmodern Culture,* a telling designation given the fact that it is supposed to define a discipline that is fundamentally aesthetic, that is architecture. For the benefit of the reader, it should be noted here briefly at least that the positions proposed within this anti-aesthetic largely stem from political ideas of the 1960s and remain far more entrenched in the discourse of architecture to the present day than we might be aware. That the concept of the "avant-garde," with all of its particular political connotations, was still the subject of serious studies in the form of new editions and translations of *Theory of the Avant-Garde* in the mid-1980s and still lingers in the standard discourse in architecture is also telling. The long arm of that legacy reaches well beyond the universities and is also prevalent among magazine editorial boards, professional associations, and building administrators working in the bureaucratic apparatus of the municipal and state levels.

However, the "critical discourse" identified above has diminished somewhat over the last twenty years. The fundamentally non-ideological and non-referential world, in which everything is possible everywhere all of the time, has a far more matter-of-fact and agile relationship with the prevalent forces that order our world than any of these critical discourses could or allowed itself to have. Rather than critiquing the economic world and its injustices, the non-referential world values its endless possibilities. For non-referential architecture, the old social ideals that made up the struggle of postmodernity of the 1960s and 1970s seem antiquated and have lost relevance in the world we live in today. The understanding that the world is disenchanted, however, prevails, at least in part, because we simply cannot believe naively in anointed authorities of any kind anymore, irrespective of their persuasion or origin. The more recent notion of "populism" in established democracies, again irrespective of its persuasion, is the most recent expression of a fundamentally polyvalent world in which long-fixated constructs dissolve. Our constructs will dissolve even more. You can lament the dissolution of ideologies but, from the vantage point of the non-referential world, it is more productive to understand this process as something liberating, as a sense of freedom and a sense of new possibilities. It is precisely the thinking based on ideological categories that was the grand innovation of modernity and postmodernity that has lost its coalescing societal power in our non-referential time.

However, these kinds of rationalizations and expressions that we see today did not lead to the complete disappearance of beliefs. After all, we are also confronted with the upheaval of Islamic Manichaeism. Even the more enlightened people of the West or East are easily prone to indulging in new beliefs that are not so much of a religious or political nature anymore but take on sociological and ecological themes instead. Still, these theories usually only stir people's imagination for a relatively brief time and will be exchanged with other ever-new beliefs that flare up at rapid intervals. Of course, these are symptoms which indeed convey that our society does not have ideals that are convincing enough for a good many people to be able to subscribe to them. Instead, we are living in a world in which there is no reference steady and strong enough to unite us. In place of relatively fixed stars that make up the heavens' tent and let us orbit around them, our wonderment when we look up to the sky is as exuberantly accepted and as quickly forgotten as the flames of a firework.

Nobody seems to be able to explain what kind of ideal our world possesses today. We even freely elect leaders who tell us that there is no ideal. The world really does not know a firmament or even something sacred any longer. It is interesting to note that this perceived vacuum is not an ideological position that one person can share or not. The absence of powerful coalescing ideals carried by powerful institutions, as was the case with the church and the state in the past, is all-pervasive. This is not a moral verdict. Any attempt to turn the wheel back is futile. In any even semi-consequential discourse today, any voice that lectures us that our time is "rotten to the core" is not taken seriously. The question as to whether we are headed in the "wrong direction" seems rhetorical at best. However, it allows us to ask those who believe in old ideals what exactly they would like to resuscitate that is respected by everyone or at least a good many? The desire to reintroduce taboos and to construct a moral argument is futile.

Therefore, it is said that we live in a pitiful, banal world that does not know anything anymore that is bigger than itself. However, such desires for a better world also raise the question: What would a non-disenchanted world look like as divisions and ruptures and breaks of any kind do not have a place in a completely enchanted world? On the contrary, we are very conscious that it is increasingly the hallmark of the non-referential world that there is no naïve reading of not only sacred texts but also of an authoritative dogma of any kind. The ambiguous and the ambivalent have taken power. The ideal way towards a single and sole truth does not exist anymore; or to put it differently perhaps, the truth is only attainable in plural form. We have not become polytheistic again but we have become polyvalent.

It is not so that the world has not learned something from the loftiness with which self-critical reason was enthroned and from the subsequent spectacle of a self-enchanted Enlightenment that brought about scientization, specialism, and fragmentation. We have learned. The world has learned that all of the ultimate questions cannot be answered in any foreseeable time. We also ask ourselves whether this situation is an exclusive characteristic of our time. Is it not possible that people can live good lives precisely because we do not possess visionary ideas, which we have become so accustomed to believing in that they have apparently made us dependent on them like addicts? Is it not possible that the interplay of magic, enchantment, disenchantment, and re-enchantment is much more enduring and valid than we might think? And perhaps also much more complex and not banal after all? People that are accused of absolving themselves from their citizenship responsibilities might be more comfortable with the non-referential: this is not the case because of a disenchantment with the world, but because of a disenchantment with world-conceptions and world-views. At the very least we can say that the non-referential world has not descended into being completely non-magical. Despite the scientization of our life, we have not transformed into pure rationally operating beings. The aesthetic has kept its fascination to such a degree that the doors to the world remain enigmatic in fundamental respects. With its independence of extra-architectural contents and its liberty from being a vessel of some moral paradigm, non-referential architecture can express—by means of its form—not only something that exists in actuality but also something that is as general as possible and as true as possible.

Genealogy of Architectonic Ordering Systems

The purpose of this chapter, "Genealogy of Architectonic Ordering Systems," is to introduce how non-referential architecture is studied. It is an introduction to how to "read" architecture, understand architecture, and how to interpret architecture. As architects, we want to study and learn from existing buildings and we attempt to make sense of them. How do we conceptualize a building? What is important for us when we encounter a building and decide to study it? How an architect studies buildings and which questions an architect asks about buildings tell us about how an architect approaches their own work.

The above-mentioned title suggests that buildings are analyzed—for a lack of a better architectural term—genealogically. This is in stark contrast to analyzing and understanding buildings socially. The genealogic analysis of a building, we could also say metaphorically, the analysis of its deoxyribonucleic acid or DNA, is the analysis of its space-constellation. It may be stated that the space-constellation—this is essentially space, how it factually exists—is the DNA of a building. With space-constellations, we refer to rooms but we have chosen to use the term space because we are referring to not only more or less enclosed chambers, the typical definition of a room in architecture, but to all kinds of exterior and interior spaces that form the totality of a building. We argue that if we study buildings, we study their genealogy foremost. Therefore, if an architect attempts to understand a building, the formal attributes of the building are what must be studied. We can surmise that the formal space-constellation of buildings contains everything that is necessary for an architect to understand a building. The statement that the space-constellation contains everything that needs to be understood is also an acknowledgment that not everything about a building can be conceptualized. The realization that not everything that we could possibly study about a building is particularly meaningful for the architect is perhaps even more important. To study the formal space-constellations of buildings is to study the inherent architectonic of a building. It brings us closer to what a building is basically about than any other possible aspect of a building that we also could analyze and draw conclusions from, such as the historical and representational contents. Studying this fundamental basis of a building is important because when we study buildings, it is not about the general deciphering of social history so as to understand the world-conceptions of one or other historical people. This is not the architect's task nor does it inform them much if the aim is to learn something about how to conceive buildings. When we point to the genealogy of architectonic ordering systems, the focus of the study is the building because the responsibility of the architect towards society is the building—the architect's competency is the building. This is not an argument for narrow-minded architects but one enabling the architect to focus on what they can control. The building is the architect's expertise and it is through the building that the architect can make the broadest possible contribution to society.

To clarify this approach: buildings are not to be studied primarily through the extra-architectural lenses of the historical and social, as is customary in academic courses on the history of architecture at universities. Buildings should be studied formally and, thus, timelessly. In other words, a building is studied as an object that does not have a time. For example, the chronological study of the course of architecture is rather unimportant if the aim is for the architect to learn about designing a building. There is no objection to students of architecture enrolling in courses on the history of architecture, and to enjoying them and learning a great deal as long as there is no misconception that such historical and social studies of buildings generate understanding of what is important and helpful for the design of buildings by the practicing architect. There is no implication here that the practicing architect should not study buildings from the past. On the contrary, the architect learns an incredible amount by visiting and studying buildings from the past and they should do so often and in detail. However, the practicing architect does not gain much at all from studying buildings as a representation of something outside themselves, namely, from studying buildings as an abstraction of an extra-architectural concept, such as religious, state, or private ideals. For example, the formal constellations of buildings are best studied without any consideration whatsoever of the "biographical information" about who erected them and why. With this in mind, it is often advantageous for the architect if nothing is known about the civilizations that erected a given building. It is actually better for an architect to not know who commissioned a building, why it was built, and what program and function it served.

There is an important difference between genealogy and history. Sometimes genealogy is labeled an auxiliary science without which history cannot be properly conducted. However, historians remind us correctly that genealogy is important but that it is not history. History, the much younger of the two disciplines, is a new branch of inquiry that emerged in the late eighteenth century and then established itself fully throughout the nineteenth century. History's objective is not the study of the accumulated information *per se;* instead, it requires a "critical approach" to the sources with a view to enabling the presentation of cause and effect. With respect to the study of a building, the historical method is less concerned with the actual formal attributes of the structure and focuses more on the interpretation of these attributes. However, genealogy remains useful for history because history cannot be conducted without it; it is its foundation, a fact that is also important for the high esteem with which genealogy is held in this tract. While genealogy was considered "only barely a science," it is also noteworthy that genealogical studies hold great sway over the popular imagination, probably more so than academic history. It may be speculated that the reason for the popularity of the genealogical is that genealogical results are less the result of intellectualization and ideological convictions and are thus far more basic. To be basic is of great value for an architect who wants to construct a building. This is the case because conceiving and constructing a building is a very basic physical undertaking. Therefore, the advantage of genealogical research is that it passes down information relatively unchanged from the source. In other words, genealogy presents basic physical facts, such as information about the dimension of rooms, the material a room is built with, the measurements of columns, the placement and size of openings, the thickness of walls, how a person enters a room, et cetera. The architect wants to know the tangible-physical-formal, in the full knowledge that there is still plenty in a building that is not quantifiable. While the tangible–physical-formal, in this sense, is basic for the practicing architect, it holds great complexities. On the contrary, historical information that a certain building is, for example, a masterpiece of a certain historical epoch because it is an exceptional representation of a certain worldview is not particularly useful for an architect; it is also not particularly useful to know who the architect was or who built it. The genealogy of architectonic ordering systems seeks out the concrete and the formal. The genealogical is useful because human beings are equipped with a basic sense for perceiving space. That ability to perceive space is not something that is learned; it is something we all share. We see this demonstrated in ancient architecture.

A very good example is the Zapotec Temple of Mitla in the Mexican city of Oaxaca. It is a good example because this building was constructed without any connection to European culture or Middle- or Far-Eastern culture. The people who built it had no contact with people of Mesopotamia, China, Egypt, India, Crete, Greece, or Rome. Through its disconnectedness from other ancient architectures, it serves as evidence that a certain system of order and the perception of space is a basic sensibility. It can be ascertained from this that architecture has ordering systems that are, in fact, universal. Of course, this does not mean that these ordering systems are made present by all peoples to the same degree—some peoples hardly built at all—but if a people invested in architecture, the use of the same ordering systems for buildings can essentially be found among peoples who had absolutely no contact with each other. Architectonic ordering systems exist independently of who built them. The Temple of Mitla is evidence of the fact that people not only perceive space but that different people perceive space identically, irrespective of the time and civilization in which they lived. Human beings perceive and assess space like they do food or music. Mitla is evidence that a genetics of space and structure exists.

We can remain with the Temple of Mitla as an example for demonstrating how a building is analyzed formally. Mitla is a case in point of spatial hierarchies and how these ordering systems coexist with each other. Of particular interest is how the two largest rooms are connected. The room with the row of six pillars is a space that is directional and conveys the impression of existing outside of the center. It is entered in the middle. The other room has four openings, each located in the exact center of the peripheral walls. The connection between the two rooms is simply somewhere. In fact, you enter the room diagonally and because of that shift, you experience it spatially. The room with the openings in all four directions feels "higher" than the one with the row of pillars. If you were to enter the room through one of the four openings in the middle of the walls, you would not experience the space as "higher." Instead, you would experience it more intellectually. It would be more a part of the absolute and of the idea—then we would perhaps only think of it as "higher" because of that intellectualization. The way it is in Mitla, you experience the room spatially and purely architectonically. The experience of these two spaces is different because you have to exit and enter outside of the main axes of these two rooms. That the hallway is a spatial sequence can be detected at the corner where two rectangular rooms make for a kind of virtual overlay. In addition, a rectangular room is comprehensible emotionally—more so than round, triangular, or polygonal rooms. The fact

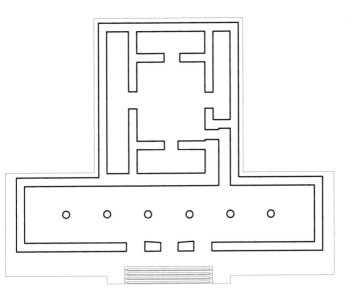

that you have to turn before entering the next room further heightens the awareness of the different hierarchies.

It would be possible to describe the Temple of Mitla very differently. We could describe and understand it as the manifestation of a philosophy, the image of a religion, the icon of a state, or as a set of personal images and ambitions. However, if buildings are studied by means of their ordering systems, the architect gains an absolute architectonic understanding of how a building is ordered. In order to comprehend the Temple of Mitla genealogically, it is not necessary to interpret it. A straightforward analysis of what is present there is sufficient. Ultimately, no names, no years, no background information are necessary to understand buildings. This example serves as a demonstration of how to study architecture: instead of studying buildings historically or symbolically or in any other referential mode, buildings should be studied formally—in other words, non-referentially. Moreover, the formal study of buildings also serves as a suggestion as to what an architect should focus on when designing a building themself.

The Idea in Non-Referential Architecture

There are two qualities that an idea for a building must have: an idea must be form-generative and sense-making. This chapter outlines what is meant by an idea that is form-generative and sense-making.

While it is not easy to conceive a viable idea for a building that reverberates in people's imagination, the expression of such an idea should not be complicated or convoluted. An idea for a building in non-referential architecture can be conveyed in one sentence, or even in just one phrase. Therefore, an idea should not be mistaken as something vague or elusive and thus difficult to express. We do not understand ideas for buildings as something esoteric that, as it were, exists nebulously and cannot be defined. Instead, an idea for a building should be exceedingly lucid. However, this does not mean that an idea for a building cannot embody spiritual and metaphysical qualities of the highest order. On the contrary, good ideas for buildings possess such qualities, as it is precisely those ideas that trigger repercussions in people's minds and souls.

The point to be made here is that, however complex and rich it needs to be, an idea for a building must be defined and described cogently, convincingly, and compellingly. An idea for a building has to be defined to a degree that it allows an architect to have logical clarity as to what kind of building they are going to design. We are not saying that the eventual building, as it will stand in front of us once it has been constructed, must be fully describable—that is impossible. However, the idea for a building must be sufficiently describable as a construct in the mind of the architect, because that clarity alone allows the architect to begin and draw a building with the consistency of a holistic construct that is based on an idea. In other words, nothing holistic can be done without an idea.

Ideas have always been the kernel of good buildings. However, the idea has gained in significance for buildings in our non-referential world. In the absence of common ideals as they existed in the past, each building that is erected today requires its own idea. Because we find ourselves in a situation in which these believable ideals do not exist in the non-referential world, the architect is no longer supplied with a set of guidelines on how to design a building. It is now the responsibility of the architect to author an idea for a building. The situation in which each building requires its very own idea is a consequence of the liberating non-referential world.

An idea, as it is understood here, is form-generative. Being form-generative is the first of the two indispensable qualities that an idea for a building must have. For example, the architect might declare that the idea is to build a secluded garden or, perhaps, a house with a public and a private room. When the idea is declared in such lapidary terms, it is not the programmatic function that defines the idea but its form-generative qualities. Every architect claims to have an idea, but what they often mean when they say they have an idea is that they can merely describe either the program or the shape of the building they intend to make. However, if an architect declares the intention to build a secluded garden or a house with two antithetical rooms, the idea describes a formal intention. The purpose is, of course, implied by its functional designation, but if an architect intends to build a secluded garden or a house for a ritual-ized life, what makes it form-generative is not the function, but, in the first case, the fact that the idea is an enclosed room and, in the second case, the fact that the idea is a place with rooms that are at once liberating and sheltering.

An idea is only architectonic if it implies a form. In other words, the idea articulates something in such a way that you can imagine a form. Ideas must be form-generating. To use the aforementioned example, it is quite easy to immediately conjure up a formal image of a secluded garden. Everybody may not imagine a secluded garden in exactly the same way as the architect does when they describe the idea to someone, but more or less everyone will have quite a defined image of a secluded garden. For example, the architect might describe the secluded garden as being surrounded by high walls, mention that there is an opening in the middle of the four walls, that it has a water feature in the center, and that it is otherwise filled with exotic plants and trees.

Contrary to such form-generative ideas, if an archi-tect states that their idea is to build an inexpensive house, this is not a form-generative idea. Such a description does not contain a formal idea. It is also not an idea if an architect says that they intend to build a white building or a small building. Nor is it an idea to declare the intention to build a house in reinforced concrete, to announce that a house is self-sufficient with regard to energy, or to proclaim that you will build a church. None of these examples are form-generative and do not, therefore, suffice as useful ideas for a building.

There is an important distinction to be made here between an architectonic order and an idea. Using the analogy of literature, it could be said here that the idea is the story. The idea is the formulation of something principled in the sense of an intention but it is not the actual devising of how a building will be manifest architectonically. Therefore, an idea has manifold ways of being ordered and subsequently formulated into a concrete building. The idea is the description of a formal intention but it is articulated prior to the conception of an order for that idea. Hence, when we discuss the idea for a building, the idea assumes a fairly specific place within the sequence of the creative process of conceiving a building. It is important to make the distinction between an idea, an order, and a concrete architectonic formulation in material terms. As such, we can surmise that, first, there is some kind of wish, for example, somebody would like a place where they can be alone. In reference to the analogy to literature, this would be the genre, for example, drama or science fiction. Second, there is the idea, for example, the idea of a secluded garden. In literature, this would be the story of a drama or a science fiction narrative. Third, there is the ordering system, for example, it is a rectangular garden that is enclosed with walls. In our analogy, this would be the plot that gives structure to the story. Fourth, we have the particular cause and effect of a story. For a building, this is the concrete architectonic formulation, for example, the material used in its construction, its color, how tall the surrounding walls are, and what kind of trees and plants will be planted in this garden. Therefore, the idea for a building is not the same as the architectural order. For example, if the architect says that their house has three walls or three columns then these are the ordering systems of the building but not the idea. To describe a building as a "house with three walls" or a "house with three columns" does not say anything about its form-generative idea.

This brings us to the second quality that an idea must have: an idea must be sense-making. We have not yet addressed the fact that not all ideas are worthy of being pursued. There are good and bad ideas for buildings. However, it is very challenging to discuss what makes for a good idea in the abstract (without having an actual task for a building at hand). Hence it cannot be our intention here to discuss what good ideas for buildings would be in abstract, non-concrete terms. Nevertheless, if an architect declares, for example, that they want to build a sphere, it is not a good idea *per se* even though the sphere does have a form and could, therefore, be understood as a form-generative intention. Instead, an architect would also have to know why they would want to build a sphere. It would then be possible to consider and discuss whether the reasons why an architect wants to build a sphere are good or bad. Other examples include those referred to above: not only is a "house with three walls" or a "house with three columns" not form-generative, the question as to why a house with three walls or a house with three columns is sense-making would also have to be addressed.

In this respect, a brief comment must be made regarding the labeling of buildings as formalism. It must be clarified that if an architect has a certain idea and this idea leads to a kind of extravagant or copious form, such as the shape of a sphere, then it is not necessarily considered as formalism. There is a tendency for a kind of wholesale attribution to label anything that has an exalted form as formalist. If an idea leads to an extreme form of a building, and that idea is sense-making, it should not, in fact, be considered formalism at all. It is important not to apply the wrong measure here: whether something is to be judged as formalism or not depends on whether the idea is sense-making or not. If the idea is nonsensical, then a spherical building is formalist; if the idea is sense-making then a spherical building is not formalism. Whether something is formalism or not is not dependent primarily on the shape of a building. Very meek buildings are also prone to formalism.

What can be stated here without hesitation, however, is that ideas exist that lead to nothing. As it is impossible to make a good building from a bad idea, introspection is needed on the part of the architect to begin anew if the conclusion is reached that an idea is bad. An idea for a building is sense-making if it provokes some kind of cognizance or insight in the mind of the inhabitant. We could call it a kind of "truth argument." The architect's idea must contain a certain "feeling of discovery" from the outset of its conception. We simply stipulate here that the idea must contain some kind of insight, something sense-making, because it is impossible to list all the possibilities about what such an insight could be. This is an admittedly broad and open-ended definition. However, it will have to remain so, as any attempt to fixate it will always fall short of all of the possibilities for new sense-making ideas. What is certain, however, is that an idea must be sense-making to be capable of stirring people's imagination. In any case, an idea for a building must be both form-generative and sense-making.

The Principles of Non-Referential Architecture

First Principle: Experience of Space

Experience of space is what a person encounters and feels when entering a room or looking at a building from the outside. This is a fairly widely accepted definition. What is less well established is that the experience of space is something that the architect conceives and creates. Indeed, we no longer acknowledge that the architect is the active shaper of an experience of space.

A widely held misconception exists to the effect that each person will have a different and completely unique experience of space when, in fact, an experience of space is not something relative, for the most part. Instead, an experience of space is something objective. It is objective in the sense of a subjective universality. What is important to realize for architects who design buildings is that for a person to be able to have such a distinct objective experience of space, it is necessary for the architect to create an experience of space with intention. The emphasis here lies on the intentional. If the architect lacks an intention for a room and the architect does not know what a person's experience of space should be like, it is highly unlikely that the visitor or inhabitant of a room will have an experience of space that goes beyond the level of a chance encounter. If interior and exterior spaces do not lend themselves to giving rise to distinct experiences—experiences that themselves enliven our imagination in a distinct way—the visitor or inhabitant of such spaces will have no other option than to either retreat with their imagination into their own private domain or to make up whatever comes to their mind. However, if that happens the experience is no longer distinct. A visitor or inhabitant could then experience and, subsequently, imagine anything and everything in the world. We argue that it matters what a visitor or inhabitant experiences in a certain room. What a visitor or inhabitant experiences is based on the architect's intention. For an architect, not having an intention for a room is gross neglect of the potentiality of what architectural space can do for people. Rooms without intentions pose a retreat from the capacity of architecture. Clearly, this cannot be the aim for buildings. Because it is a given that the architect can no longer rely on preconceived ideas, in non-referential architecture the architect must author the intentions for the distinct experience of space in any given room of a building.

It is necessary that the architect conceive experiences of space. The architect does so by giving a room a precise physical formulation in terms of its shape and its walls, columns, floor, ceiling, material, light, texture, acoustics, and all of the other qualities that engage a person's senses on entering a room. A consequence of this demand is that the architect must already have an intention in mind before the building is drawn up. The architect must have an idea for the building. From the idea for the building, they can deduce the intention for any given room. In other words, the architect must know what kind of experience of space the room will trigger in the inhabitant before they draw the rooms for a building. By now it is abundantly clear that the experience of space is not something that "just happens" when a visitor or inhabitant enters a room. Therefore, one can say that the architect proposes a kind of thesis when they conceive a room—it could be referred to as a "thesis on the experience of space."

An important delineation must be made from the outset: the experience of space is not only a visceral feeling that an inhabitant somehow senses in their stomach—the often invoked "gut feeling." The inhabitant encounters a building with the totality of their sensory apparatus, including their cognitive powers.

The mind is part of the physical apparatus of human beings. Buildings are not experienced emotionally and through feeling alone—that is, not just viscerally. Instead, thinking is part of the physical experience of a building. Buildings that are perceptible through emotions and feelings alone leave people on the outside with little room to engage—people are left alone with their emotions and feelings. This is an often-misunderstood aspect of architecture: it is assumed that a building that is experienced emotionally is inclusive. Precisely the opposite is true. Architecture that aims to be perceived foremost emotionally is actually the least social architecture. Such an architecture tends to be private; it is limiting and not very interesting. On the contrary, architecture should seize and grip people. In order to take a hold of people, you must also engage their minds.

If it is stated here that the experience of space is not solely a visceral feeling, it does not mean that there is not also a phenomenological dimension involved when dealing with the experience of space. This is pointed out here very deliberately because the so-called phenomenological approach to architecture is all too often understood as meaning that the architect must somehow retreat from their responsibility to create an experience of space. Writers and critics who claim the phenomenological mantle for themselves stress the experience of space as something that is seemingly "created" *post-facto.* They claim this—based on their hermeneutic conviction—because they assume that perception is almost entirely based from within the mind of the visitor or inhabitant. This is incorrect. Rather than understanding the object-subject relationship of building and inhabitant as being played out almost solely in the mind of the perceiving inhabitant, the experience of space is something the architect creates with the physical facts of a room. Therefore the architect is the active shaper of the experience of space— at least as much, if not more, than the visitor or inhabitant.

In view of what has been stipulated above, an important epistemological foundation in architecture must be reasserted: the experience of space is something we would like to call a "basic feeling."

This basic feeling is common to all human beings. The understanding that experience of space is indeed common to all human beings is something that has been lost to a large extent in recent times. It is this loss of understanding that the experience of space is a basic feeling that is responsible for the impression that the experience of space is not something that is created by the architect but something that every inhabitant creates for themselves.

The experience of space is understood as a basic feeling in that all human beings have more or less the same impressions when they encounter the same room. Epistemologically, these "unfiltered" or immediate impressions of the physical facts of a room account for almost our entire experience of space. That is not to say that we do not also interpret rooms based on subjective mental and physiological filters. However, it is a misconception to believe that these subjective connotations that each person brings to their own interpretation fundamentally alter what is perceived when we encounter a room. For example, if a member of the indigenous Eskimo people, who has lived their entire life in the northern circumpolar region of our world, and a member of the indigenous Berber people, who has lived their entire life in the Sahara Desert, encounter the same room, they will essentially have the same experience of the space. If an Inuk and a Berber enter a Gothic cathedral, they feel the same upwardly soaring experience of space, even though they have never seen such a space ever before in their lives, and their respective backgrounds would not prepare them to feel that way. Their experience of space is given by the distinct physical qualities of a spatial arrangement as a person finds it in a room—its shape, form, material, light, texture, acoustics, and everything else that makes a holistic room. In other words, it is the totality of the formal qualities that are primary for a person's experience of space. Of course, such a claim does not mean that every person's experience of space is absolutely identical. Past experiences and the differences in every human's physiological apparatus will give rise to some degree of variation, however these variations are not the decisive and deciding factors behind how we experience a room. When we present the basis for architecture, it is important to accept that the experience of space is something absolutely fundamental and basic to human beings.

If we were to compare the experience of a building's space with a movie, the interpretative experience of space based on a person's past experience and physiological apparatus could be compared with the special effects of a movie—not much more than that. However, it is clear to everyone that the special effects are not decisive for the movie as a whole, that is for the movie's story and plot. The special effects can vary without altering the story of a movie. This comparison presents an important delineation that is true for buildings: the experience of space possesses a certain logic and that logic is subject to the architectonic idea. The experience of space is not primarily something we stumble on incidentally and in a quasi-animalistic way, and then each human being makes up his or her own experiences. Rather, and to use the analogy of movies once again, the experience of space is intentionally directed by a writer—someone who authors the movie. Not unlike the author of a movie, the maker of an experience of space, the architect that is, is also an author.

If you experience a room with all the senses— including the common human desire to interpret a room—then many different visitors and inhabitants will come to the same conclusions about a room. They will have a very similar experience of space of that room. We can also underscore the point of a common experience of space with an example from the art of music, which will make the argument about the fundamental feeling of the experience of space abundantly clear. Rooms and entire buildings, in fact, are not unlike musical compositions. The way two listeners feel about a sonata by Bach or a symphony by Beethoven has little to do with whether one listener grew up in the Arctic region and the other in the African desert. The aural impressions of these pieces of music will evoke more or less the same basic feeling in the two listeners. If the musical compositions are played accurately as written in the score by the respective composer, this will be true not only for these two listeners but for all listeners. When we listen to Beethoven's Ninth Symphony, we all feel about the same. To return to architecture, the same applies when people encounter the Taj Mahal at Agra—everybody has more or less the same experience of space on seeing that building.

It is psychological and physiological aesthetics (first formulated in the latter part of the nineteenth century) that allow us to understand space and form as the "raw materials" of architecture. These particular aesthetics suggested a way of liberating architecture from content-carrying images. Inadvertently, the same psychological aesthetics appear to suggest that the experience of space is now somehow less tangible and less common to all people. This is a significant misunderstanding. It is essential to clarify that this inadvertent degradation of the common experience of space is nothing more than the relativist misinterpretation of what was, in fact, intended to be an epistemological elevation of aesthetics through the subjective capacity of human beings. It was never intended to result in its relativist abolition. To clarify this misinterpretation: the famous proverb "beauty is in the eye of the beholder" never intended to stress that one beholder might see something in one way and another beholder in another way. Instead, what Immanuel Kant meant by stating "beauty is in the eye of the beholder" in reference to the words of Thucydides was that human beings ought to use their eyes—the emphasis lies on the use of the eyes and not on the multitude of interpretations by the beholders—so that they can make a judgment about what they see. This is referred to as a subjective universality. It is subjective inasmuch as a human being is actually doing the seeing; it is universal inasmuch as a human being will see what it actually is, namely something objective, if that human being uses their inherent capability to see. The subjective and the relative are two very different things. The relativist "twist," whereby each beholder sees whatever they feel was never the intention and it poses a far from slight mis-understanding that has had very unfortunate consequences—in architecture too. Applied to the experience of space in architecture, subjective universality means: if you sense a room sufficiently well, various observers, namely the visitors and inhabitants, will come to the same conclusion about what it is actually like. Most people, however, understand subjective universality to be an oxy-moron. The fact that subjective universalities exist legitimizes the capacity of architecture to aim for a specific experience of space that is conceived by the architect. The failure to do so does not fulfill the inherent capacity of rooms, buildings, and architecture as a whole.

For the reason outlined above, the experience of space of a room is not a question of education; instead, it is basic and common to all human beings. In the introduction, we referred to Alberto Giacometti's statement to the effect that the best thing about his sculptures is that you can touch them. We also wrote that such immediacy is the best thing about buildings, namely, that you can physically experience their rooms. In the context discussed here, this also means that a highly educated astrophysicist senses approximately the same thing when they inhabit a room as someone who never received any formal schooling at all. Anyone who ever watched the reaction of people entering the Abbey of Le Thoronet in the Provence region of France can attest to this, as it is unlikely that all visitors to the Abbey are astrophysicists. Hence, the experience of space is not an intellectual skill but a basic capability that all human beings possess irrespective of their education. That the experience of space is a basic feeling does not mean, however, that the experiencing of space does not originate within a human being, in the sense that it is a sensual experience of the human mind and human feeling. As psychological and physiological aesthetics have demonstrated, the experience of space is born within us, but that does not mean that a given room does not trigger the same impacts in the minds of all human beings, irrespective of their educational or cultural background.

The fact that an architect must know what kind of room he or she is going to design is also important for the creative process. An architect must know what kind of room it is going to be before fabricating the first drawing. The projecting of an experience of space should not be misconstrued as a search for an experience of space. Indeed, it may take more than one attempt to find the correct formulation for a room and to obtain the imagined experience of space conceived by the architect in their mind. However, the architect who knows what qualities the rooms will have does not design by means of a search for a solution. Instead, their approach is about the correct implementation of the idea. In contrast, an architect who does not know what qualities a room should have will design by means of some kind of search and hope to eventually arrive at something pleasing—although in such cases the architect is not really sure what that might be. This approach is not advisable. Unfortunately, this kind of search is all too common in far too many architecture schools, where it is introduced as a legitimate way of designing buildings. It is madness to think that architects could begin by merely making a more or less indeterminate sketch and a room then emerges somehow, in some kind of additive manner, out of which an experience of space will finally result. Such a way of working would only lead to a kind of animalistic, or, to use the more fashionable term, an "incidental" way of conceiving an experience of space. It is quasi-animalistic because it does not involve much more than stumbling upon whatever these incidental spaces would lead to. Such rooms could easily be referred to as "found" rooms and as a "found" experience of space. This contrasts with conceived rooms based on an idea and an intended experience of space.

When discussing the experience of space, there are two other noteworthy characteristics that should be touched on briefly. It is important to realize that rooms exist in relation to other rooms, not unlike a symphony, in which there are typically a number of movements. Rooms and their relationships with other rooms in a building can be compared to such movements. They belong to a larger whole but they also have relative independence. If you occupy one room of a building, you tend to remember the other rooms too; accordingly, you attempt to construct continuous interrelationships. It is one of the major tenets of modern architecture to attempt to create consonance in our heads when we imagine inter-relationships between rooms. Using the above analogy with a symphony, there is the attempt to conflate all movements into one continuous composition so as to manifest the wholeness of the piece. Of course, non-referential architecture is not against that aim of arriving at some kind of a whole, oneness, or totality *per se.* However, we do not rely on consonance to manifest totality, because this model is untenable and too simplistic for the non-referential world that we know today. While we do know that the world as such is one entity, it is difficult to conceive of an alignment of all of the representational things—including build-ings—of our world under a single rule. To apply this understanding that not everything exists under a single rule (a rule should not be mistaken as the idea) to the discipline of architecture, it is not of any advantage for our experience of space if all rooms have a structural ordering system that is aligned into a unifying consonance. The two rooms of the Temple of Mitla, which were described in the introduction, could not exist as they do if the rule of unifying consonance were to be applied. In non-referential architecture, rooms are consciously "cut off" from each other so that no or only very limited consonance can be attained in the inhabitant's mind. Non-referential architecture does not aim for consonance. Instead, from room to room, it requires a break in the sense of a *caesura.* A *caesura* is understood as a conscious break in the flow of a spatial experience, a kind of a pause marking a precise differentiation from one spatial configuration to another. Contrary to the paradigm of consonance, in this instance changes in room configurations are not gradual but abrupt. Such *caesurae* create contradictions, yet these contradictions are kept in mind as you go from room to room. In these moments, the experience of space is not solely a "gut feeling"; it involves the memory of what we have already seen and felt when we approached a building and walked through its rooms. Such experience of space speaks to the creative imagination of human beings, that is something more than the imagination that is animal-like and always lives in the presence alone. Such experience of space fosters speculation. Even if you know a building well, such experience of space offers the inhabitant the possibility of assembling and re-assembling their "life rituals." Such experience of space invites the construction and reconstruction of even common everyday life— of the seemingly most basic and mundane daily habits and actions. Such an invitation to a fundamental construction of everyday life with regard to the experience of space makes such spaces non-referential, as they are independent of images, traditions, customs, and moral questions. It is a basic reconstruction of our life's rituals and as such, it is a liberation.

Finally, it must be said that the experience of space is not only independent of a specific building material but it is also independent of images and certain forms. It is the architect who must decide what kind of experience of space a given room should have. For example, they must decide if it is an introverted room or an extroverted room; and such qualities are independent of material and form. If an architect attempts to design an extroverted room, they can do this in any given material and in any given language of architectural expression. As such, the selection of the building material with regard to the experience of space is a personal one and one made by the architect. What the architect should consider with regard to the experience of space is the sufficient complexity of experience. A sufficient complexity of experience can be attained in any material. However, it is advantageous to attain this sufficient complexity if a room, or better an entire building, is made from one primary material (e.g. steel, reinforced concrete, or timber). The fact that you define, and thus limit, the means with which you create any given room or building has the benefit of increasing the complexity of the experience of space.

Second Principle: Oneness

Oneness has implications for the conception of space in architecture. As such, the exterior and interior spaces of buildings are subject to "an architecture of dividing." This is contrary to buildings whose spaces are the result of additions of geometrical shapes. It is impossible to create oneness through an additive-compositional mode. In other words: a whole cannot be made out of parts. The only possible way to end up with a whole is to begin with a whole. Oneness requires the declaration of the building as a system. Such a system is subject to one idea for that one building. For the purpose of demonstrating that a building is a "oneness," architecture can be separated into two groups. There is one kind of conception of space that understands space as one and then divides that space until it works as a building. The other kind is a conception of space that begins with nothing and then composes a building by adding parts. The former is "an architecture of dividing," the latter is "an architecture of adding." These are two fundamentally different conceptions of space, and it goes without saying that they are not of equal value for architecture. Only the first kind allows for oneness. Moreover: only the first suffices for non-referential architecture.

As long as society shared a view of the world that was relatively fixed—we could say as long as we imagined our world as having originated from some sort of center—the idea that buildings need to be

72

conceived as oneness did not arise as a principle. The demand for oneness—oneness is not necessarily synonymous with unity—only came into the foreground when the vestiges of common societal values segued into a fully polyvalent and non-referential world. While the conceiving of a building as oneness was always formally superior to that involving an additive-compositional process, prior to the advent of the non-referential world, it was not absolutely necessary for buildings to be a oneness, because the societal currents within which such buildings existed were consolidated enough to provide anchoring. The existence of a building could be justified by its mere belonging to one ideology or another. Buildings already had an assured place in the world because they were more or less referential expressions of common values of a society that lived in that world. This is no longer the case. Today, each building exists for itself. Spatially and ideationally, buildings have no other choice today than to be conceived as entities that contain everything but also possess unlimited possibility—a oneness.

What does it mean when it is stipulated that buildings must be a oneness that contains everything but must also possess unlimited possibility? When we say that a building contains everything, it refers to the fact that a building is formally a completely organic whole, in which every element is subject to the governing idea for that building. It is what we physically encounter with our senses when we are outside and inside a building: the walls, floors, ceilings, openings, material, construction. A building must contain its form under that one idea. That is one aspect that makes a building a oneness. The other aspect of how a building is a oneness is through its sense-making possibilities. The two aspects are linked inasmuch as a person's distinct experience of space in a room also makes the person creative about possibilities at the same time. Such possibilities imply space. A building is a oneness if there is a relationship between contained rooms in the physical domain and the possibilities for expanding yourself in the meta-physical domain.

With respect to the fact that a building must also engage a person metaphysically, it was stated in the introduction that the best buildings trigger a discourse between the "here" and the "there" and between the "I" and the "unknown." In other words, the best buildings foster a discourse between the presence of one individual human being occupying a room for themselves and our simultaneous taking possession of the brittle limitless space that we call the universe. Because we have fought hard to obliterate any foundation and firmament that stood between these two poles as a society, our immediate habitation, in the non-referential world that is, is now tasked with helping us to bridge the two realms. With all the changes that have arisen in our society, what has remained the same is that we need shelter for our existence, not only physically but also metaphysically. Martin Heidegger once said: "The work erects a world." In the same sense, when we say that a building must be a oneness, the rooms that an architect designs not only shelter the inhabitant from rain and sun but also allow for the construction of a home for the self in the brittle world of the metaphysical kind. The fact that such ideas are not exclusive to philosophers is evident from the following statement by the painter Barnett Newman: "Life is physical but it is also metaphysical—only those who understand the meta can understand the physical." This is also the task of architects. The architectonic room is arguably not only the most obvious form of architecture, the inhabiting of rooms is certainly among the most basic and also most common experiences of human beings. The room has always been there. Rooms attain their exceptional position because almost all people dwell in them. And because almost all people dwell in rooms, it is there that the architect finds the limits for the spatial conception: the simultaneous presence of the universe and I. To conceive space in such a way is not new *per se.* A holistic oneness is already implied etymologically in the term "room." The word "room" comes from the Old English *rum,* which, not unlike the German *Raum,* denotes "space." Both words—room and space—stem from the Latin word *rus,* which means "open country"—in other words, the universe. Variations of the relationship between "room," "open field," and the act of making space are present in many other languages. To conceive a "room" for a building is at the same time also a making of "space" for oneself in the world. To conceive a room is at once the most basic technological act but also the original act of containing our metaphysical homelessness. These are seemingly timeless aspirations of architecture. Nonetheless, what is new compared to earlier times is that a building cannot be a symbolic image in order to then delegate the actual metaphysical work of connecting us with the so-called higher realms to the endeavors of religion, politics, and science, not to mention to faith, ethics, and logic. Such delegating was possible until very recently. But these intermediaries have lost their power. Today, rooms themselves must trigger the creativity of their inhabitants. Rooms can do so because the experience of space is a basic feeling that precedes any conceptualization. This is the undisputable power of rooms defined by walls, floors, ceilings, openings. However—and this is the rationale for the principle of oneness that extends from the physical to the metaphysical—a room is also a state of mind. A room is a place in which you are alone with your thoughts. It is a space in which you are with yourself.

As outlined above, there are different conceptions of space. In fact: the demand for oneness challenges the prevalent conception of space that views it as an additive assembly of parts. It has been pointed out already that "an architecture of adding" is a compositional conception of space. Moreover, such an additive-compositional conception of space is geometrical in a most fundamental way, namely, it is not only geometrical in the sense of composing shapes in architecture but, beyond that, it is also geometrical in the sense of causing disjunctions into an either-or logic of thinking and imagining. In philosophy, and in our general understanding of things, there is the tradition which thinks of a concept as a kind of compartmentalization that circumscribes all of the entities to which the term refers, for example, "white" refers to all possible white things, "table" refers to all possible tables. But, based on this, everything is reduced to a disjunction (a kind of boundary): you are either inside or outside the conceptual compartment. This mode is geometric in the most fundamental way. It makes not only the metaphysician but all people think that outsides and insides exist in nature when, in fact, they do not. This mode of operation also works with parts when, in fact, there is only a whole. We conclude that such a geometry-based conception of logic also does not support a conception of space aiming for oneness. It must be interjected here that, despite the overwhelming presence attained by this geometrizing mode of thinking in modernity and the fact that a great many people—including architects—cannot imagine of conceiving space in any other way, it is a specific and not self-evident conception of space. That there always were alternative conceptions of space, even when it seemed that there was no other way, is evidenced by some of the great masterpieces of architecture that could not have been conceived with a geometrizing logic. Buildings by Francesco Borromini come to mind and, of course, the entire oeuvre of Ludwig Mies van der

Rohe. The architecture of these two architects has little to do with geometry. For example, nothing substantial can be learned in an analysis of the German Pavilion in Barcelona if it is approached with a geometrizing mindset searching for compositional principles, because contradictions that are not subject to that logic and to that associated conception of space are pervasive throughout the building.

That the non-referential world demands a different framework for conceiving space is not, therefore, something plucked entirely out of the sky. One of the earliest challenges was tied to the philosophical approach of phenomenology. The phenomenological discourse in architecture held orthodox modernism responsible for an organization of architectural space that led to a "loss of being" and countered it with an "inhabitable geometry." This challenge to orthodoxy implied that, rather than relying on abstract rationales, such as geometrizing disjunctions, which tend to be removed from the immediacy of the inhabitants' life-experiences, spaces of buildings should be based on experiences that will directly stimulate. Because such a critique was difficult to transpose for practical use, architects often understood architectural phenomenology simply as a remedy against the supposed "coldness" of functionalist architecture with its propensity for utility and efficiency. Architects reacted by putting forward a supposedly phenomenological approach that invites tactility. While this was a partial response to the fact that the subjective response to the objective presence of architectonic space is a basic feeling that is present prior to any analytical category, buildings became increasingly conceived as an assembly of various kinds of materials—a kind of a three-dimensional collage—consisting of stitched-together momentary narrations and storytelling in the attempt to overcome seemingly uniform and exclusive modern architecture.

A subsequent thesis proposed that our contemporary world requires a method in which contradictory meanings can exist—a model of thought that became known as "deconstruction"—that reacted to an ever more fluid and less fixated understanding of the things that make our world. Peter Eisenman spearheaded a discourse of what this could possibly imply for architecture. He called for architectural form that necessitates a complete substitution of semantics with syntax and would then allow us to perceive form simply within a matrix of differences.

A half a century has passed since deconstruction entered our discourse. Its findings have been largely absorbed by society, mostly without any conscious knowledge of them. The impact of deconstruction on the non-referential world that we live in today cannot be overestimated. However, with regard to a spatial conception in architecture, deconstruction was also less successful. Even though these findings of deconstruction implied that our way of conceiving space is too much in the habit of making undue reductions, its architectural exponents did not ultimately seek the oneness that its underlying theory actually suggests. As a matter of fact, deconstruction remained stubbornly faithful to geometrizing models of conceiving space—notwithstanding that it made great efforts to dislocate and superimpose spaces with sometimes contorted operations. We can speculate why this remained the case. Perhaps it was precisely the allure of new tools and instruments, namely the ability to shape three-dimensional curved surfaces by means of vector-based calculations with newly available computer applications, that ultimately hampered the breakthrough. While its propagators were inclined to believe that deconstruction needed to deal with space differently, their didactic experiments in architecture emphasized the fracturing of oneness rather than oneness itself. However, it is testimony to the overarching current of the polyvalent non-referential world that—even if they come from supposedly opposed poles, such as phenomenology and deconstruction—architectural theories ultimately aimed for the same thing: the dissolution of the reduction of the experience of space inherent in a geometrizing system that operates by establishing disjunctions of being either this or that. However, the advent of the fully polyvalent and non-referential world has changed things fundamentally: architectural phenomenology and architectural deconstruction were dedicated to meaning. Non-referential architecture, on the other hand, is unconcerned with meaning—it is concerned with possibilities.

To be spatially conceived as a oneness has very direct consequences for how a building exists in all its aspects, including its form, its construction, and the material with which it is built. Above all else, in non-referential architecture the building exists for itself in such a way that we can state that a building segues into the world. Buildings are no longer exemplifications of ideals. Instead, the equation has made a 180-degree turn: the rooms of buildings construct our lives and, accordingly, our world in the most fundamental way. As a consequence, because they cannot rely on extra-architectural meanings, buildings in non-referential architecture also segue toward absolutes. This is the rationale as to why a building requires an idea in the first place. With regard to its physical presence, it is the idea that makes a building a oneness. Everything in a building exists under the rule of that one governing idea. In very straightforward terms, a building is constructed as one thing and appears as one thing; ideally with no construction joints, no parts, and a single material. To view a building as a oneness liberates it formally, materially, and constructively from the fixed semantic connotations that we typically assign to buildings and rooms. Suddenly questions such as "what is inside," "what is outside," "what is the top," and "what is the bottom?" become challenging basic questions for architects that are not simply functional or constructive in nature. Instead, these questions about buildings and rooms and how they are constructed are acts of fundamental ground-laying of something new in a state that is liberated of references, images, and symbols—in other words, they are non-referential.

One of the implications of conceiving rooms in such a way is the liberation from style-architecture. For example, the definition of the traditional façade tripartite of plinth, middle part, and roof frieze and of the different degrees of rustication of a façade is debunked as the remnant of what it is today, namely a theory of ornament based on defunct semantic connotations. Instead, what is decisive in terms of whether a building is a oneness depends on how the walls and floors are built. If a building is not supposed to appear like a collage, the emphasis is not on the expression of constructive measures for creating boundaries and thresholds. Indeed, walls are conceived not unlike a frame that stands in space as a kind of ideational scaffolding. While such a conception of walls and floors does not absolutely dictate that both sides of these building elements are constructed identically, it would be ideal if it were so. Moreover, constructing all of a building's walls and floors in the same thickness also enhances the oneness of a building. What is true for the appearance of a building's walls is also true in the vertical direction: if all floors have the same height, the building is perceived as a oneness and not as something that is stacked up from individual floors. If the room heights of the ground and top floors are different to those of the remaining floors, a building appears if as if it were made in parts. Different room heights are also undesirable because this demonstrates that buildings are conceived on the basis of their immediate functionality and not of a more general formal idea.

Long-standing compositional ideals and theories of ornament, such as the so-called classical order or the theory of tectonic, are obsolete. The way rooms are constructed is not aimed at a particular expression of an architectural language that is based on references, images, and symbols. Instead, it is the presence of the building in a purely physical state that stands in the foreground. What holds true for the liberation from the fixed semantic connotations of the classical order or other tectonic theories also applies to the use of materials with which buildings are constructed. Aiming for buildings as oneness also tends to liberate materials and construction techniques. For example, it liberates us from assumptions that certain materials should be used in the interior and others in the exterior of buildings. Of course, there are good practical considerations for this based on the material attributes and how materials are used. However, these determinations are not as fixed as one might assume, nor is it particularly advantageous to think of them as fixed for buildings that need to trigger repercussions with inhabitants in our non-referential world. Most materials and construction methods can be used in many more ways than is customary practice. The usual practice of constructing walls, floors, and roofs is based at least as much if not more on semantic traditions than on technical limitations. As has already been stated, it is the exchange of the semantic with the syntactic that offers people the liberation of the non-referential world so that they can think their thoughts in the corresponding buildings.

Third Principle: Newness

Only a building that is new—a building that embodies a quality of something that has never been present before for a person in the way that they encounter it—has the power to rouse their power of imagination and to captivate them. We state unequivocally that architecture must strive for newness. Newness is understood as an aspect of novelty, of a basic experiential cognition in a formal architectonic sense. In contrast, even if a building is well conceived and built with great constructive competency and skill and, perhaps also, with great technological innovation, but does not have newness, it should only be considered as a mere work of craft. A work of craft, even if it is exceptional craft, is not enough to fulfill architecture's ultimate social task, namely to engage people in a dialog and discourse and to make people creative.

It is not possible for a building in a non-referential world to trigger engagement without aspects of newness. As such, this is not different to the way things were in the past. Newness has always been important for architecture. Buildings that rouse people's imagination always have something new about them. While it was always the case that newness was desirable for architecture, the demand for newness has become much more acute in our non-referential world. This demand has become more acute today because buildings have no other choice than to be viable independently in a non-referential world. Independence is not understood so much in the sense that a building is a solitary object but in the sense that a building has an effect on us in terms of our way of life and our quality of life. A building must be independently viable today because it cannot rely on a given ideology at a time when such ideologies are not believable to people anymore and thus lack coalescing power. Therefore, more than ever before, buildings must be independently viable—and to be viable they must have an aspect of newness. It is through newness that they become liberated and gain independence. It is through newness that they engage people. And it is also through newness that buildings have the power to modify people's expectations and viewpoints and thus transform lives.

Newness is not understood as synonymous with progress. The task of newness is not advancement and improvement in the sense of any kind of development, technological or otherwise. A building made out of stacked stones and nothing else can still be new today in the sense it is presented here. For lack of better terms to describe it architecturally, newness is of an epistemological dimension. Newness is a fundamental component of how architecture engages people. Ultimately, newness is of ontological importance for us.

In contrast to this unequivocal recognition of newness for architecture, many new buildings are justified solely on the basis that they belong to an ideology. Many new buildings are defended as worthy by architectural critics because they correspond with certain ideologies or so-called "schools of thought." A hefty dose of proselytizing still occurs in academia, architecture journals, and other forums with a view to promoting a specific kind of architecture in line with ideological models. This is an untenable situation in a non-referential world, in which no significance can be gained through subscribing to ideologies. Rather than ascribing great value to buildings precisely because they fulfill prescribed and predetermined expectations, it is an aspect of newness that it touches people in a certain creative way that is fundamental and precedes any critical legitimation.

It is precisely this societal task and role of architecture—to make people creative—that is the ultimate reason why buildings must have aspects of something new. Therefore, newness has a specific task in architecture. Newness is the initiator that provokes the viewer of a building to engage in a discourse with the building and, therefore, with the world. Without newness, viewers will simply leave a building by the wayside, as they do with all buildings that do not contain something that engages them.

It is, again, the architect who assumes the responsibility for designing something that contains newness. The architect is the shaper of that newness. This is no simple task. Newness requires a kind of a philosophical moment inasmuch as architects expose themselves to a thesis that must contain aspects of newness. In other words, through buildings architects create a thesis about man's relationship to the world. This thesis, if we want to call it that, must be new. Unfortunately, newness in architecture is often derogatorily associated with the fashionable. However, newness has little to do with the fashionable. It must be realized that it is not possible to work on a thesis that has already been dealt with sufficiently. Not unlike philosophers and philosophy or physicists and physics, architects and architecture require the continued renewal and extension of a thesis in order to push the quest regarding the limits of our discipline. Newness is what makes philosophy, physics, and architecture—to stay with these three examples— creative and, therefore, also relevant. Hence, the creative quest ends as soon as an architect stops seeking newness. In this instance, architects could just as well stop working altogether. The task of designing buildings that do not carry an aspect of newness and are not, therefore, much more than utilitarian shelters and are at best well-crafted structures can be delegated to architects, who either are satisfied to view their role as that of building facilitators or craftsmen; otherwise, the making of buildings can be delegated entirely to builders. There is no need for an architect if newness is foregone. Therefore, a thesis must bring something new to the fore: a thought, an idea. Not much can be accomplished without a thought or an idea that embodies something new. Newness allows for a kind of "thinking ahead"; and it is precisely through the provocation of something new that human beings become creative. In that sense, newness provides a positive moment, a kind of an inspiration, and it is that mental constitution of the new that allows viewers—not just architects but anyone—to be creative. Everyone feels such creative inspiration when they come across buildings of this kind.

A few more things must be said about newness. The first point about newness is that it must be differentiated from today's popular "lifestyle" trend, which has also enshrined a kind of newness in its banner. The newness that is intended here excludes the entire spectrum of the "lifestyle" trend popularized under the general heading of "wellness"—which includes incessant visits to galleries, museums, and concerts as well as other learning experiences dutifully embraced by the *Bildungsbürgertum,* the educated middle class. When newness is evoked, the aim is exactly not to succumb to such "lifestyle" experiences but to seek newness of the kind of ontological moment that touches deeply rooted existential questions concerning our place in the world. This is a very important distinction. The "lifestyle" movement's notion of newness is the product of marketing. It is a technique that was appropriated by the field of architecture relatively recently and with the help of which the architecture of recent decades gained popularity and justified its right of existence and worthiness. The kind of newness that is sought after in such a propagated "lifestyle" of renewal and rejuvenation is in the realm of entertainment. In any case, it has nothing in common with the power to fundamentally transcend people's existential expectations and viewpoint by offering them a new framework for sensemaking.

Another important point about newness is its timeliness. The issue here relates to how timely a new building can be so that people are able to engage with it creatively. Newness is not timeless. The following description of how the work of two particular architects has been received is indicative of the tenuous and difficult role of newness in the reception of architecture not only within our profession but also in the world-at-large. It is noteworthy that Frank Gehry's architecture has been subject to a very different reception to that of Antoni Gaudí. Gaudí's architecture was considered bizarre at the time when he produced his work. In contrast, despite all the discussions about the merit of Gehry's architecture, his work has never been labeled as naïve and bizarre nor was it, for that matter, labeled as particularly fashionable. Instead, Gehry's architecture has always been taken as a serious contribution and his work is understood as significant for society. Now, this may be a very unjust assessment of Gaudí's work, as his work is clearly not without merit. It could be argued perhaps that the fact that Gehry's work was received well while Gaudí's was largely rejected when it was built tells us something about the world we live in today. The point to be made here is the following: it is of utmost importance for an architect to understand the prevalent societal currents of the world in which they work so that they can assess the degree of newness that engages people creatively.

On one level, the acceptance of Gehry's work and the rejection of Gaudí's can only be explained by an increased heterogeneousness of our society. It can be argued that if Gaudí's work were to be built today, it would also be celebrated. Indeed, it may be said that this is the case when we consider the long lines of visitors in front of Gaudí's buildings in Barcelona today. Of course, Gaudí's current popularity has little to do with a more serious discourse that his work would merit and has, alas, everything to do with the above-discussed "lifestyle" movement. However, it is not Gaudí's fault that our media-driven society is enamored with images but uninterested in discussing how these images affect people.

On a more consequential level for newness, the fact that Gehry's work found admiration as soon as it was built does suggest that Gehry had an exceptionally keen awareness and understanding of what degree of newness the people of his time would be able to absorb with their own powers of imagination and, subsequently, use as a reference in their attempts to wrestle with their own existential questions. This was not the case with Gaudí. Most people were puzzled by his work and found it bizarre. Gaudí's work did not "speak" to broader societal currents when it was built. Therefore, we can surmise that an architect must be very astute and know how far they can push the sensibilities of the people of their own era so that these very people are still capable of engaging creatively with their buildings. It is very likely that Gehry's architecture would also have been labeled as bizarre had he designed it in Gaudí's day. As he has skillfully demonstrated, Gehry's idiosyncratic formulations of architecture are tolerated today. The fact that Gehry was able to judge his times correctly and that his work was not rejected as being bizarre and absurd speaks directly to his capability to understand nascent societal currents, like the previously invoked sniffer dog who senses how far it must go to get to newness. To be able to do so is arguably the most difficult social competency required of an architect.

Therefore, the most important topic here in relation to newness is the architect's capability to access society's sensibilities so that they can conceive a building that has just the right amount of newness. Architecture should never be bizarre, nor can it be desirable for people to begin to associate buildings with the bizarre. It is an important and difficult question for architects to establish where exactly these demarcations happen to lie at any given time. These boundaries are constantly shifting and require a fine-tuned awareness of the current world on the part of the architect. The architect must know the world very well, otherwise they cannot creatively define newness. Needless to say, our non-referential world, in which architects are given very little guidance on what to do, makes the demand for newness even more challenging. But that is the task at hand: the architect has no other choice than to somehow become very attuned to the currents of the world; the architect must indeed become not unlike that sleuth who can design buildings with aspects of newness of such a degree that they become actualized just prior to the moment when these architectonic formulations become acceptable to a sufficiently large segment of society. Once these formulations have become fully accepted and known to most of society, they have already relinquished their epistemological power to rouse people creatively. This process is accelerated today because digital communication enables everybody to see everything instantly. This sensitive and highly calibrated capability to know your own world is the foremost reason why society needs architects and how society benefits most from having architects. Accordingly, we can state that the ability to define newness architectonically is the foremost social task of the architect.

There is yet another important point to be made when we talk about newness. When demanding newness, you might ask from where such newness would originate. The answer is: newness in architecture comes from architecture itself. While it is clearly possible that architecture and buildings can be influenced by any kind of extra-architectural parameters, such extra-architectural inspiration would have to be adapted to the domain of the architectonic as immediately as possible. Newness in architecture must play itself out formally, not historically or symbolically. In other words, newness in buildings cannot play itself out analogically. Newness is formal in the sense that it is the physical fact of how a building exists in the world—its shape, its rooms, its structure, its material, its construction—and how a person encounters that formal constellation of a building. Newness in buildings is encountered as a very basic experience of space and not as an intellectual explanation.

Therefore, when we stand in front of a building or inside a room, the new is not an extra-architectural appliqué imported from outside of architecture. Newness plays itself out in the experience of spaces in all their mental and visceral possibilities and not by detour of grafting abstract and intellectualizing non-architectural themes onto buildings that exist in the realm of the symbolical or historical. It is best for a building to be purely architectonic, but if the difficult detour outside the architectonic is taken, then any such extra-architectural influences must be integrated into what is fundamentally architectonic: into the realm of the formal—into the physical properties of a building as it exists in the world.

One strategy, which would have to be considered a folly, would be to take a route that leads outside of the domain of architecture and to then construct bizarre importations of the extra-architectural into buildings—however meaningful these extra-architectural qualities might be in their respective fields, be it in mathematics, sociology, politics, art, or any other kind of endeavor. It is easily imaginable that the stream of more or less meaningful importations is endless, but such extra-architectural "thematizations" of architecture tend to be banal and rather boring when used in the realm of a building. They almost never expand the limits of architecture itself and are even less often beautiful. Such buildings made by means of extra-architectural "thematizations" remain episodes for the discipline of architecture. Only if such imported "thematizations" are made fully architectonic—that is when they have become fully formal—do they lend themselves to further adaptations by the sensitive and creative minds of the people. Ultimately, architecture does not require extra-architectural themes for newness. Instead, architecture itself is the subject from which newness arises.

One final aspect of newness cannot be forgotten: newness demands authors. An originator is required for newness to arise. Without authorship, there would be no newness. And while newness requires authors to come into existence, it is also a fact that the architect requires the new to achieve mastery of architecture: it is only by creating something new that an architect can truly demonstrate and prove how good they are. Here too we can say: without newness, even the best-crafted work of architecture will qualify its creator as a technician but not as an architect.

Fourth Principle: Construction

Buildings benefit if they are constructed of one single material. To construct a building with a single material presents the formal intention unequivocally. This assertion is based on three considerations: first, a building that is made from only one material is ideational in any sense; second, in a building that is based on an idea, it is the architect's task to decide on the material with which the building is built; and third, the single material defines the formal qualities of the building.

Old buildings were largely built in a single material, mostly either in stone or timber. Today, it is often argued that it is no longer possible to construct buildings in a single material due to complex technical, environmental, and legal requirements. However, there is evidence that it is still possible to construct technically highly complex buildings in a single material today.

When we look at old buildings—for example, the Basilica in the Apulian city of Ruvo—we see a building that is essentially built of stone. There are some other materials present, such as the wooden doors, and there is also some glass; the stone roof is also covered with terracotta tiles for protection. However, it is essentially a building made of one material. The Abbey at Le Thoronet has a similarly concise material palette. Even the roof there is made out of the same stone as the walls and floors. Similar yet even more radically succinct materialization can be seen in Fatehpur

Sikri, a city in the Indian region of Uttar Pradesh. These examples are provided here to indicate what is meant by constructing a building out of one material. Yes, there are other materials present but these mainly relate to the apertures. Other than the materials used for the apertures, these buildings are built entirely with one material.

The rationale as to why it is desirable to construct a building in a single material is new, however. To construct a building with one material helps to achieve a kind of distancing-effect. The distancing-effect strengthens the appearance of the building as a result of an architectonic idea. To construct a building with one single material aids the non-referential inasmuch as it liberates the building from the entire array of semantic associations, images, and attributes that we tend to read into buildings simply because we are familiar with them. To illustrate this point: if the entire front façade of the Basilica in Ruvo, namely its pilasters, portals, Lombard-band, ornament and everything else, had not been built in a single material but in different ones, the architectonic idea of the building—in this case of enormous weight pushing down to the earth while there is a big room inside—would not be understood. If the Basilica were built with several materials, it would be impossible to feel and comprehend the idea of heaviness and the open room because multiple materials would dissolve and differentiate the idea. Even more dramatic is the example in Fatehpur Sikri: the fact that all buildings—each of them unique—are built in the same red stone emphasizes the idea of the unification of the many. The distancing-effect moves the idea of the building into the foreground of our perception. Thus, the constraint of one material is, in fact, a liberation. In the case of Fatehpur Sikri, for example, the distancing-effect of one material allows a building to become formal while consciously de-emphasizing the attributes of material and construction. It is only in the realm of the formal that a human being can think and imagine freely. Therefore, the rationale as to why a building is best constructed in one main material is primarily an epistemological one. It is particularly necessary to liberate a building from semantic connotations in our non-referential world so that people can occupy these buildings freely and think their thoughts freely. Moreover, the commitment to a single material makes a building more coherent structurally and constructively, precisely because materials have attributes.

The decision to build a building with one material or other is ultimately the choice of the architect, because there is no causal relationship between idea and material in the same sense that there is one between idea and order. It is important, however, that the choice of the material by the architect is still deduced from the idea for the building! Deciding on the material with which a building is mainly built is not unlike selecting a language with which a story is told or a text is written. To remain with this analogy, in many cases it would be possible to write a given text and describe the same plot in one language or another. However, the language with which a text is written changes the text. The same is true for a building. For example, it is possible to design an introverted room or an extroverted room in either steel, reinforced concrete, or timber, but, needless to say, these rooms would look different. The structural concept would also be different. It is the freedom of the architect to select the language that they speak, but it is also the architect's task to decide on a material for a building—that material becomes the basis for the building's formal qualities. It is not the case that an idea must always be implemented with only one and the same material. For example, if the idea is to build a secluded garden, it can be defined in various materials. However, this choice is a limited one: the architect's choice is guided by that fact that a building needs to be built in the one material that gives it the ability to transport the idea for that building.

For example, concrete has the attribute of being a "casted material." Thus, it would not make sense to cast in concrete a building whose idea requires a modular (composited) form. On the other hand, it is the very nature of brick that it always results in something modular, because a brick is a small, typically rectangular module. For example, it is nonsensical to build an irregularly undulating shape in masonry. Therefore, to some degree, the choice of a material for a building is a personal choice of the architect but that selection should not be mistaken for an unencumbered one. Therefore, we can say that an idea does not just demand a material, it also requires materialization in a specific material. Needless to say, a material choice is not only not completely personal, it is also not primarily a consequence of technical and economic considerations. It is also important to note that the dimensions of a building limit the material choices.

However, rather than amplifying the choice of one material or other for a building, it is more important to emphasize the importance of the fact that an intentional choice must actually be made. It must then be stressed that the material choice must bring utmost consequentiality. If an architect stipulates that he or she conceives a building in timber, steel, or reinforced concrete, it should mean something. In other words, if an architect declares, for example, that a building is being built in timber, then it ought to be a building that is fundamentally built in that material and exploits the inherent possibilities of timber in all its characteristics. It is very unsophisticated to declare a building as a timber building and, for example, have the joints made out of metal. In this case, it is no longer a timber building because the material attributes of timber are removed with the addition of metal in precisely the part of a structure that is crucial for making a timber building exactly that, a timber building. As a result, a building becomes a mere jumble of materials—with the loss of the sought-after distancing-effect and the failure to fulfill the aim of making the building a liberated formal construct.

Even worse is the complete absence of an intentional declaration as to the material with which a building is being constructed. We can also say that buildings with many materials and without a recognizable main material are testimonies of the absence of ideas for buildings and the most direct evidence of their futility. If no decision is made for a particular material, the outcome is usually a building with multiple materials that compete with each other. In this case, the material-specific attributes of these different materials will "fight" and offset each other.

It is all but impossible to build a coherent formal whole with a jumble of materials. Of course, in some cases, assemblies of different materials, which make buildings look not unlike showrooms at building material exhibitions, are used as a language for expressing the importation of concepts like "multiculturalism" or "democracy" and other non-architectonic concepts. Needless to say, such an approach is problematic.

Buildings without the necessary material and constructive consequentiality become unidentifiable jumbles because they make everything seem possible. All materials and their inherent attributes then compete with each other. It is only a slight exaggeration to say that the less clear the architect is about his ideational intentions the more materials will be present in such a building. One can add to this verdict that, in most cases, material joints and changes of materials in buildings occur either because of an absence of a coherent idea for a building or because the architect in charge does not possess the necessary ability and material knowledge to construct a building stringently. In this case, the jumble of materials is simply a demonstration of the architect's lack of ability in the technical devising of a building.

Since this is a book primarily aimed at practicing architects, now is a good time to state that the architect must be able to construct the building they conceive. Too often, the architect is more or less absolved from the tasks of constructing and overseeing the actual erection of the building. "Constructing" here refers to the technical devising of the project before it is erected on the building site. "Overseeing" the actual erecting of the building refers to the architect's supervision of the building contractor, craftsmen, artisans, and technicians. The architect cannot succeed with only a rudimentary technical knowledge of building science. Instead, the architect must be a *virtuoso* equipped with a technical knowledge of construction to a degree that it enables them to be in complete command of how to implement and execute an idea for a building. What is needed here is not just a passive knowledge that allows an architect to intervene when a problem arises. On the contrary, the technical and constructive expertise of the architect is crucial when they begin to conceive and draw up a building. The technical and constructive knowledge of the architect is of fundamental importance: the architect can only be innovative and creative and achieve aspects of newness in their buildings if they have this high level of technical and constructive expertise.

It is simply not a successful approach if various engineers, technicians, builders, craftsmen, and artisans discuss the construction of a building among themselves without the architect playing a decisive role in all the meetings. It is the architect who instructs everybody else. The widespread custom whereby the architect is a designer who is removed and not in control of the technical devising of the construction of a building and the subsequent erection of the building has a direct and visible effect on the quality of buildings. An architect cannot control the growth and development of a building if they are not present and in charge.

The final point to be made under the heading of construction concerns the crucial importance of statics and structure. It is not unheard of for buildings to be conceived simply as a shape or a shell and entirely without a structural concept. However, it is really all but impossible to work with a coherent architectonic idea while not knowing the specific structural concept of a building. Therefore, not only should the structural concept of a building be conceived by the architect, it is a fundamental part of the architectonic ordering system, right from the outset when an architect gives order to their idea for a building. The approach whereby a civil engineer simply takes the architect's design and inserts a structural concept retroactively and somehow "makes it work" rarely results in satisfactory buildings. No oneness will come about if structure is not integrated into the architectonic order from the outset. The structural concept is already manifest in the ordering system. Together with the shape, rooms, material, and construction of the building, its statics concept and its structure form an organic whole. Only the exact placement and the dimensioning of the building elements is the responsibility of the engineer but not the structural system as such. In other words, the architect conceives the structural system of a building when they conceive a building; later on, when the structural system is already in place, the engineer will calculate the exact dimensions of the building elements.

Fifth Principle: Contradiction

Contradiction is defined as two or more parts that require each other but do not require each other at the same time. From the outset, it is important to point out that a contradiction is not an opposition of two or more parts. Instead, a contradiction is a compositional strategy that grows organically from within the building. Contradictions are also not dualities, as it were, of black and white; rather, to stay with this analogy, a contradiction is something in which black and white would occur simultaneously, yet not as conflation or collage of the two. By no means is a contradiction something that is instigated by adding something to the buildings in order to create a contrast—for example a contrast intended to deliberately prompt a particular kind of interpretation.

The following example can help to explain what is meant with contradiction: imagine you enter a room in a small building. Once inside, you find a staircase. Human beings do not typically contemplate how a building is laid out. In this case, a person entering that room and seeing a staircase assumes that there is something upstairs because they see a staircase. This simple and straightforward conceptualization is so common that we do not even realize that we are conceptualizing the layout of a building. It is so common that the process is carried out effortlessly to such an extent that we can arrive at a conceptualization at once.

Here is a similar yet different scenario: a person enters that same building but now there are two staircases next to each other. Something quite different now occurs in that person's attempt at conceptualization. They will ask: What is going on here? What am I to do with two staircases? Where should I go? Does it matter which staircase I take? Will I get to the right place on the floor above? While the attempt at conceptualizing the building with one staircase was completely effortless and seemingly second nature, in the second building, the process of moving from the sensory stimulus of encountering two staircases towards imagination and then attempting to conceptualize is not simple at all; it is most likely that it cannot even be completed fully in the person's mind because they are confronted with a contradiction.

To have two staircases that lead upstairs from one room is a simple example of a contradiction. It is a contradiction because we already have inadvertently construed the building on approaching it. We assumed that a staircase exists to access the second floor. In this example, the person will resolve this contradiction of the existence of two stairs in their mind only after they have walked through the building. It is only then that the person will be able to "figure out" the building with respect to the two staircases. Later in this chapter, it will be argued that the very best contradictions are those that never can be fully conceptualized. Many kinds of contradictions are possible. They can involve any part of what makes a typical building, such as the structural concept, materialization, apertures, the plan of the building, constructive measures, movement through rooms, or the approach to rooms. Contradictions are planned by the architect and are part of their creative and innovative capability and skill.

The above-presented example also reiterates a point made earlier: namely that nothing is added that is not inherent to the building. The building just described requires a staircase because there is a second floor. It is a necessary element. It is not a "contrast element" that is inserted to illustrate a didactic moment. Contradictions are not subversive. If an unnecessary and new element were simply inserted for that reason, it would not work as a contradiction. People would just see it as something that is foreign and does not belong. In other words, again, as something subversive. It would be understood as an otherness. At best, they would see it as a contrast. However, to work with contrast is a rather banal and unsophisticated compositional strategy that has nothing in common with contradiction as it is understood here for the purpose of non-referential architecture.

Aristotle once made the distinction between difference and otherness. A contradiction presents itself at first glance as a difference, as something that does not quite fit together in people's attempts at conceptualization. A contradiction is a kind of "fissure"—a sort of *caesura*—that triggers ever-new attempts at conceptualization because the difference is such that people imagine ever-new ways of how they could deal with that difference. Contradictions stimulate and make people creative. We can also say that a contradiction is a compositional strategy relating to how a building becomes sense-making.

Contradictions, as such, do have a didactic dimension in themselves, but not in the common "educational" sense. Contradictions are not there to teach something specific about a building. It may be added here that architecture, like all artistic endeavor, should not be educational *per se.* However, people do like to think and figure things out in a more or less mentally playful way; and sometimes they even like to engage in ontological thoughts about their place in the world. Accordingly, it can be said that the aim is to gain true discernment from contradictions: first, as contradictions but then as the two poles of a oneness. This is the kind of didactic dimension inherent in contradictions.

Therefore, inasmuch as a building is a didactic "instrument," a contradiction is something of a tightrope walk. However, a building must make people creative over and over again, as once people have figured out something, they put it aside. Once a person has conceptualized something to a degree that they can simply apply it for further reference—because that person knows everything about it—it has lost its creative appeal. Contradictions are also important for newness. People enjoy attempting to comprehend something they have never seen before or have never experienced before in an agreeable and determinable way.

Contradiction as a compositional principle is not dissimilar to the system with which Immanuel Kant attempted to explain what triggers people to arrive at a judgment that something is beautiful. Kant argues that there are three phases that come into play before people judge something to be beautiful: first, there are the sensory *stimuli* activated when a person is confronted with something; second, the initial stimulus triggers a person's imagination; and, third, there is the person's attempt to conceptualize what has been imagined. Kant argues that a sense of beauty arises not if a person is capable of absolutely conceptualizing something in the sense that they completely "figure it out," but by the constant going back and forth between ever-new possibilities of imagination and ever-new attempts at conceptualization in the person's mind. The best art, and supposedly also the best architecture, is the kind that is able to continuously engage the person's mind between imagination and conceptualization. It can be imagined like a game of ping-pong between imagination and conceptualization.

Kant claims, therefore, that a person would be bored if they could comprehend something fully. They would no longer deal with it creatively once they have conceptualized it. If this happens, the only thing left to do is, perhaps, to apply it for further reference; however, the actual aesthetic riddle would be solved and, thereby, lost. The paintings of Abstract Expressionism, the work of Mark Rothko for example, can be used to explain this phenomenon. If somebody were to stand in front of a painting by Rothko and then come to the conclusion that they fully understand the painting, they would never look at it again in that same way because it is now a fully conceptualized quantity. Obviously, however, if a work is completely inaccessible for people for whatever reason, it also will not trigger the desired aesthetic experience. This is why we refer to the tightrope walk and why the window for a successful work of art—in our case a building—that achieves the right stimulus of our sensory apparatus is a very narrow one.

Needless to say, such contradictions speak to the sensibility of people who live in a non-referential world. Non-referential architecture denotes but it refuses to explain or narrate, and it leaves behind any vestiges of a theatrical mode of persuasion and propagation. Non-referential architecture and its contradictions allow a person to harvest sense despite the fact that there are no more fixed semantic associations as existed when we made sense of the world by means of a referential system of relatively fixed contents of images and symbols.

Another case of a contradiction is a building whose shape appears to be really banal in the sense of an absence of an academic gesture: for example, if a building assumes the most common shape of a house: a house with walls, windows, a door and a pitched roof, as we know it from thousands of children's drawings. There is nothing speculative about what an architect would have tried to accomplish with the shape for such a building. It is just the most normal and common shape of a house. However, if something is then superimposed on such a house that does not typically belong to it, it can result in the generation of unbelievable profundity out of that simple shape of the most ordinary house. For example, on entering such an archetypical house—that at first glance presents to us as the quintessential sheltered home—we might discover that it does not have a roof. The seemingly perfunctory house that we took for granted can then suddenly become enigmatic. We are confronted with a condition that liberates the house because new possibilities are opened up to our power of imagination: a visitor will wonder about a house without a roof. Therefore, the contradiction of the familiar with the superimposition of something very unfamiliar, leads to a transcending of the seemingly banal or routine to achieve something profoundly sense-making. There is a distancing effect.

Needless to say, the point of contradictions is not that houses can simply have no roofs, for example. Contradictions must make sense for a well-functioning building. Contradictions are not a gimmick; they only become viable and powerful if they are part of a perfectly operating building organism. However, if a visitor enters a building and they discover that, for example, three quarters of the building are not enclosed because there is no roof, they will begin to think creatively about the sheltering function of the house. They may begin to contemplate that a building's shelter is not just achieved with a conventional roof, and that shelter from the universe also exists, even if a person would not be protected from the rain and the sun. Such a contradiction may trigger the consideration of what is involved for a building to be a home and what exactly it is that ultimately shelters us. A person may be confounded by the fact that large parts of a building do not have a roof. Such a building might appear nonsensical to some people, but for others it might trigger existential and metaphysical thoughts. Therefore, having given the matter some consideration, a person might arrive at the conclusion that it is sufficient for only one quarter of the building to be covered, namely when they notice that their comfort has not been reduced but rather extended by the lack of a roof. The fact that three-quarters of the building are not covered might become its most treasured quality because the inhabitant now has a very direct physical relationship with the heavens' tent. Is there anything more sheltering than overcoming our metaphysical homelessness? Contradiction is an important compositional principle for making architecture today; it is a strategy for creating buildings in a time when fixed meanings are no longer shared while also aiming to make people creative.

Another kind of a contradiction is what Gottfried Semper formulated as *Stoffwechseltheorie.* This term describes the process of a transformation that results from the change from one material to another. Semper attempted to describe the relationship between timber architecture and stone architecture and was seeking extrapolations towards an architecture in iron. Applied to our epoch of non-referential architecture, the transformation from one material to another is no longer in keeping with the positivist historical process in the Semperian sense. Instead, such transformations can go in any direction. For example, a contradiction based on such a material transformation emerges if a timber house were constructed in concrete. Similarly, it is a contradiction if a stone building is constructed in the form of a timber frame building. This is precisely what was done in Fatehpur Sikri. Such transformations read as contradictions and liberate buildings from all their inherent connotations. Mentally, you have to radically realign yourself with everything a building is about because references have either vanished or are recognized as invalid.

Sixth Principle: Order

Architectonic order links the idea for a building with the built architectonic actuality. Hence, the architectonic order is how the idea is first conveyed into form by means of building elements: the formation of walls, floors, roofs, openings, and columns amongst each other within its ordering system. These primary elements make the order present. In other words, the idea for a building is first articulated by an ordering system. The ordering system is eventually given a material manifestation, a distinct material-physical presence, in that its walls, floors, roofs, openings, and columns are actualized in material and construction. Therefore, we can stipulate that the architectonic order of a building is the bridge between an architectonic idea and the physical actuality of a building: idea—order—building.

The interrelationship between idea—order—building implies that the architectonic order is a deduction of the idea. An order is a transcendence of the idea in the sense that order is conditional on the idea. To stipulate such a causal relationship between idea and order—and to a lesser extent also between idea, order, and building—is diametrically opposed to such notions as "incidental space," "incidental form," and "found architecture." There are two basic ways of establishing order: one is deductive and the other is inductive. These two methods have always been adopted by architects, albeit not typically with scientific rigor to the extent that we would like to suggest that the conception of a building amounts to a method in the scientific sense. Nonetheless, the distinction between the deductive and the inductive has assumed critical importance for non-referential architecture. We say that: the deductive approach alone makes sense for the definition of the ordering system in non-referential architecture.

The inductive, upon which the "incidental" and the "found" are based, has no grounding in the non-referential world. That it is no longer possible to work inductively in a world that has striven to become polyvalent and has thus relinquished any relatively fixed principles—as existed in the modern and postmodern periods—is seemingly self-evident. Notwithstanding the fact that the notion of "truth" is increasingly fluid and shifting, the inductive is only useful as long as it is embedded beneath a firmament of "truth." Still, modernity and postmodernity, in particular, were defined by a belief in the value of shared ideologies. Under the umbrella of those ideals, modern and postmodern architecture could search inductively and be content with "found architecture." This is no longer the situation we find ourselves in. It is precisely because of the absence of a principled foundation that non-referential architecture necessitates the deductive approach. It is, therefore, the idea for a building that is deduced in non-referential architecture. However, there is a second explanation for the rationale as to why order can only be the result of the deductive: the ordering system cannot be self-referential. The ordering system in non-referential architecture is non-referential, not self-referential. As a matter of fact, in today's architecture, it is this latter case leading to buildings based on the "incidental" and the "found" that produces apparent emptiness and deserves our focus. Self-referential and inductively derived architecture that is not subject to an idea does not present a thesis or a premise that strives to be "right." Instead, it only presents either strong or weak probabilities that are not the results of a thesis or premise but are the generated order of an abstract and more or less complex nexus of various processes and factors. The inductive approach that leads to "incidental space" aims to generate buildings using more or less coincidental parameters, such as the boundaries of the plots, infrastructure conditions, functional needs, material attributes, and the building code. Such parameters are insufficient for an architectonic order to be sense-making.

Conceptions such as "incidental" and "found" are problematic. To accept the "incidental" and the "found" as a creative way forward for architecture equals a declaration of intellectual and artistic bankruptcy, in that its propagators retreat from the idea that a building can, in fact, be something sense-making. The recent elevation of the "incidental" and "found" as an acceptable mode of design invalidates the understanding that architectonic order is an outcome of an idea for a building. The approach of making a building by means of the "incidental" and "found" insists that architectonic order for and by itself—and devoid of a link with an idea—gives a building its sense. However, the order that can be created by the inductive search for the "incidental" and "found" form is coherent but not sense-making. This is a fundamental difference. It is the same as admiring the clockwork of a watch for its own sake without considering what it is supposed to do. A clockwork can be exceptionally beautiful on its own, but it is an undeniable human fact that we seek to find it even more beautiful, if we can also somehow link it to an idea—to use the clockwork analogy, namely, that we know that the clockwork measures time and, ultimately, that it links us to the very idea of time. Clearly, the architectonic order for a building is much less specific than a clockwork with regard to a purpose, yet buildings, too, cannot be devoid of sense-making ideas.

The idea that ordering systems should be made inductively—resulting in the aforementioned "incidental" and "found"—is a recent phenomenon. This trend is most likely an outcome of an ideology that has led us to become much more comfortable with and accepting of the inductive approach, probably because we think of it as participatory—a kind of "grassroots process." The inductive approach is a method that also could be understood as a "bottom-up logic." We appear to think of the inductive as more engaging than the so-called "top-down logic" that is associated with the deductive. The deductive might be less desirable because it overtly admits that it requires an author—an individual architect for example—to assume the responsibility for defining limits and intentions and establish rules. The inductive method, on which incidental ordering systems are based, is the antonym of the intentional, the deliberate, and the projected—all attributes that appear important for the making of buildings. However, the accidental, casual, coincidental, by-the-way and chance approach that is associated with the incidental appears to have a certain allure in the search for the expression of architecture. Moreover, the inductive approach purports, if not to say claims, that decisions are no longer made by an author or individual architect. Nevertheless: at some point in the process, the inductive search still requires judgments and decisions on the part of the architect to do things in one way or another.

Normative definitions tell us that deductive logic is defined as the process of reasoning from a premise or a thesis to reach a logically certain conclusion. On the other hand, inductive reasoning is defined as reasoning that derives general principles from specific observations. Deductive logic links a thesis with conclusions. In the case of a building, it links an idea to an order. Speaking in a strictly scientific manner, it can be stated that if all premises of the thesis are true, the variables or terms are clear, and the rules of deductive logic are followed, then the conclusion reached is necessarily true. Of course, as architects, we tend to think that the projection of a building—in other words the "throwing forth" in the sense of conceiving or "giving birth" to a building—is in the realm of the artistic and aesthetic and we are, therefore, highly uncomfortable with such a strict application of logic to our work. However, when we say that deductive logic links a thesis with conclusions, it means nothing other for the making of a building than the fact that an all-encompassing idea governs everything for the making of a building. Therefore, what we deduce from an idea prevents each decision made by an architect from being situational.

The inductive approach suggests that a building somehow grows without intention; moreover, it pretends to be a way that is controlled by nobody. In this way of working, the building does not demand a sense-making idea. If we believe in the viability of working without an intention, we must imagine that the architect sits in front of an empty white sheet of paper and simply begins to draw something on the paper. Or architects begin to design by building various kinds of models. It could be anything. This approach is perpetuated in a great many architecture schools where students are asked to "simply begin." Such an approach relies solely on the hope that the architect receives inspiration while they sketch, draw, and make models. Yes, the more skilled an architect is and the more means an architect makes available to themselves, the more sophisticated their drawings, sketches, and models will be. Nevertheless, the sophistication of a more elaborate process with ever more resources does not fool anyone about the fact that only something incidental can result from a non-intentional inductive approach. In this approach to the formulation of an architectonic order, we are made to believe that rules would be "found" inductively from the study of ever more specific conditions. However, this approach is not rectified by the production of the maximum possible sample size so as to justify the conclusions, because an analysis alone does not bring forward a sense-making intention for a building. Indeed, it invalidates the premise that authorship has been superseded by a process that is supposedly more logical because no individual makes decisions and judgments.

It is known that almost anything can be analyzed somehow and it is also possible to derive some order from it. However, the existence of an order alone is of no value. And even if such an order is considered beautiful as an object, people who encounter it will typically want to be able to make some sense of it by extending it to something that matters to them. The attempt to forgo the rationality of a deductive intention and, in exchange, to inductively rely on a kind of *objet trouvé* does not bring forward a sense-making order. Instead, it is nonsensical. It is nonsensical because a solely internalized, you could say, mechanistic complexity devoid of any humanistic sense-making relationship cannot serve as the legitimacy for a building. Not unlike a device without a purpose, such buildings will simply not speak to people. While non-referential architecture is liberated from fixed images, symbolisms, meanings, and references, such liberation cannot be the result of mechanical processes, notwithstanding the complexity of such processes. The ordering system for a building ought to be non-referential, not self-referential.

However, the inductive approach to designing a building is not all futile and useless. Once an architect has conceived an idea for a building and has then deduced an order for the building from that idea, the inductive way of working becomes useful. We imagine that some other relevant decisions for a new building that are not necessarily causal are also made deductively, for example, the decision regarding the material with which an idea for a building becomes manifest. Hence, there is a point in the process of making a building when working inductively becomes reasonable and fruitful. For example, it seems reasonable if the architect works inductively in recognition of the attribute of a material that they have chosen to build with. As one possible outcome of an inductive way of working, the attributes of the material will bring corrective certainty for possible structural concepts. Therefore, the designing of a building occurs in a twofold and seemingly contradictory approach: in one direction, the architectonic idea regulates the making of the building deductively, and thus guides the architect in their decisions about what needs to be done, while in the other direction, the material and other parameters define the building inductively, and thus control and limit the possibilities of how a building can be constructed and built.

The knowledge, discipline, and mental agility required to know when and how to work deductively and when and how to work inductively is very important and should be disassociated from any ideological questions such as a preference for a "bottom-up logic."

If we address the constructive facts of a building, its making is not a philosophical or political act, but rather pragmatic in the sense that it is the wrong moment to be bound to a specific approach simply out of ideology. In fact, making a building has absolutely nothing in common with ideology. Non-referential architecture takes advantage of both deductive and inductive ways of working. However, what is important in the discussion on the principle of order is that—without doubt—order is the result of an intention that is set forth by the architect in terms of how they imagine the building to be—even though the non-referential world we live in is highly skeptical of all things "top-down." It is precisely the non-referential condition that demands intentions on the part of architects. An order is deduced from the idea. The ordering system for a building is intentionally decided on by the architect because the order for a building is the embodiment of something that makes compelling sense to the people who use the building.

Seventh Principle: Sensemaking

Buildings must be sense-making. A building that solely embodies a conceptual order is nonsensical. The quest for the sensemaking of a building is inevitable.

Proclaiming sense-making as a principle of non-referential architecture may seem unexpected. The non-referential and sense-making are not typically seen as having something in common. Such an assumption is incorrect. Non-referential architecture can be sense-making.

There is a tendency in contemporary architecture to retreat from the sense-making capabilities of buildings. It is argued that sense-making is no longer possible in a world in which there is no accord on the viability of references. While sensemaking for the majority of stakeholders in the field of architecture—who typically have not yet accepted that we live in a non-referential world—remains an approach by which the sense-giving occurs through the introduction of one or the other extra-architectural importations into buildings, those who have realized that the non-referential world exists have reacted by eschewing sense-making for buildings altogether.

An approach emerged recently—from precisely the above-described situation—that reduces a building's "truth" to a solely internalized and hermetic coherence. Very often that internal coherence plays itself out with great rigor in the form of the result of various parameters that an architect decided to adopt. The best of these kinds of buildings are beautifully and ingeniously calculated and materialized artifices. However, the zeal of the most rigorous conceptualization of parameters, and the subsequent inductively established ordering systems of these buildings, cannot conceal that they lack what is essential about buildings, namely something sense-making that would be of concrete relevance to people's lives and their dreams and desires. Instead, however ingeniously worked out and technologically sophisticated they might be, buildings gain through their sense-making capabilities because they offer a framework for creatively overcoming the metaphysical homelessness that people seem to feel more often than not in today's disorienting non-referential world. This is why it is not enough to simply establish an order. Order as such, is not sense-making.

The remedy for those who eschew sensemaking is to adopt an inductive approach that leads to "incidental" and "found" ordering systems. Such ordering systems imbue buildings with coherence. Those who embrace this approach argue that, nowadays, coherence is the sensemaking in architecture in our non-referential world. This is shortchanging the possibilities of architecture. The conviction of only working conceptually (we have mainly used the term "inductive" rather than conceptual so far in this text) towards an order—even if the order is coherent—does not guarantee sensemaking. On the contrary, an order is only a means to sensemaking. To illustrate this point:

while there is agreement that $1 + 1 = 2$, this sum is not sense-making beyond its mathematical logic. Only when we assign some humanistic values to these numbers do they gain significance in life. An exclusively coherent architectonic order can be comprehensible but it does not generate anything: it is comprehensible but not sense-making. It is not enough to merely be touched by architecture; the architectonic order must be something concrete about the life of a person.

Architecture is more than the subject of a logical order. Instead, the effect of buildings exists in the domain of aesthetics. For example, if the order of a building is a circular plan with a domed roof, the order of such a building only becomes magnificent if it embodies the transcendence of a humanist idea.

Of course, geometry and mathematical paradigms are also the outcomes of humanistic ideas, and numbers do mean a great deal. In this particular example, the dome is architecturally sense-making not only because it is the embodiment of the idea of heaven, but also because the dome was made possible intellectually by the idea that the number 0 had a newly received value, possibility, and limit all at once—attributes that were inconceivable, for example, in the earlier culture of Ancient Greece. Thinking inductively about stone and statics would almost certainly never have resulted in a dome; and if it had done so, it would not have provided a framework for sensemaking for the people who encountered it. The number 0 was the intellectual expression of a form-generative and sense-making idea that emerged two thousand years ago and led to the architectural invention of the dome. We surmise, however, that the dome was present prior to the mathematical paradigm shift, because spatial embodiments of ideas typically occur before their intellectual conceptualization. When someone says that $1 + 1 = 2$ today, stipulates that a building has eight columns, decides that a building is a square, or that a building has three walls, these orders cannot stand alone—those ordering systems must also be somehow sense-making. There is a tendency to think that the reduction of order to something solely coherent yet not sense-making makes buildings rhetorical. However, buildings cannot be just a clever ordering system and, therefore, exist solely as vessels of a kind of rhetorical truth, a type of truth that is self-referential and myopic. The logic of a building—in other words the search for a truth—must always be an actual search for truth. While it might be a disenchantment with world-conceptions and ideologies that led to our non-referential world and its hallmark disbelief in authority, the world has not become entirely non-magical. The quests of our lives and world are no less an enigma than they were in the past. The fact that we are not inclined to accept one ideology or other does not mean that the order of architecture is not always in the realm of life. The task of architecture is to set life in a spatial order. In short: architecture distills and sublimates the idea of a life in one way or another. The building is not a mechanical process of an abstract order but a formulation that is sense-making. The aim of sensemaking is to extend one's possibilities. Through a building, life is felt physically as a formation and experience of space and, in that way, it is a confirmation of life as such. When it stands there in reality, a building is creatively sense-making through the empathy of its viewer and their creativity of interpretation.

Fundamentally new today, and different from the past, is the fact that a building must be sense-making, first and foremost for the people who use it. Sensemaking is very particular inasmuch as an individual person physically experiences a particular space that is sense-making. Also new today is the fact that sensemaking is different for every building. The fact that sensemaking is different in every building, yet that it is a principle nonetheless, is especially important.

We are no longer used to embracing principles in our polyvalent world. In our non-referential world, we tend to think of principles as an oxymoron. However, this is not so if we do not conceive of the principle of sensemaking as the subject of ideologically fixed semantic images and symbols. If we let go of our preconceptions in relation to viewing the world historically and view it formally instead, we realize that sensemaking defines the world fundamentally. Sensemaking is not bound to a particular theory or ideology. In its fundamental way, sensemaking is primarily the concrete appearance of sensory knowledge. It could be referred to as "great reason," again, a kind of reason that is formal rather than historical. Buildings need to be sense-making so that human beings can order their lives in the most fundamental ways. Such activity is creative and becomes a function of a logic that precedes any conceptualization and any ideology. Sensemaking is the principle of architecture that deals with the question as to the why. The question as to why something is a good idea must be answered by the architect. In one way or another, the Experience of Space, Oneness, Newness, Construction, Contradiction, and Order are based on the question as to the how. Sensemaking is based on the question of why. While the principles as they have been placed in this text should in no way be understood teleologically, namely, in the way that one principle builds on the principle that precedes it, it is correct that order, space, rooms, material, construction, and composition are all subordinate to sensemaking. Sensemaking is not unlike the glue that holds everything together that is important for a building.

In the absence of an example of a concrete building in the process of being designed, it is difficult to discuss exactly what sensemaking is for a building. Nonetheless, it can be said that not everything that comes to the architect's mind is sense-making. If an architect proposes one thing or another, it must be reasoned whether it is sense-making or not. For example, if an architect designs a building in the shape of a cube, there must be a discourse

128

regarding the sense-making rationale for doing so. To state it in this way seems almost lapidary, but after the first moment of contemplating the task, it becomes evident that it is challenging to design something that is sense-making because it is not possible to engage a person creatively if an aspect of newness is not also present. This is particularly true today, as architects cannot rely on a preconceived semantic architectural language. Today, the architect must author sensemaking out of the blue sky, in the sense that there are no ready-made formulations available to them. In other words, the architect must invent the sense-making architectonic formulations.

Architects in our time find themselves involved in a search for a "truth argument" in a world without belief in truths. It is exactly the predicament of having to create spaces and rooms that are sense-making in a world that requires the architect to have a profound insight into the fundamental currents of the world so that buildings do not succumb to the rhetoric of formalism. It is too lofty to say that an architect must have something philosophical to say, but they do require the determination for a thesis conveying a discovery that creatively enlivens the mind of a person. Truth is a difficult quality to come by in our time. And as unsatisfying as it might be for those people who are believers in a truth, in the sense of a religious faith, and those people who do not accept any claims to truth at all, there is still a realm between those two extremes in which most people find "truths" that are important and useful for their lives. Perhaps we must be satisfied in our time with something being "as true as possible" rather than the absolute truth, which, by the way, only ever existed in the domain of faith, as even philosophy, for example, "only" deals with wisdom. Still, the dictum of "as true as possible" is much more desirable than a "rhetorical truth." Buildings of non-referential architecture benefit from these kinds of "truth arguments."

Sensemaking in the sense of being "as true as possible" requires a moment of understanding. If we accept that we want to understand something, it follows that we must also accept something that we refer to as truth. Yes, truth is a treacherous territory in a world that no longer appears to have any common ideals. However, it is precisely because non-referential architecture cannot rely on fixed preconceptions for buildings that there must be a kind of "truth argument," not entirely unlike in a philosophical treatise. As a "truth argument" is understood as a search for a truth, a thesis—if one wants to call it that—as fleeting as that search for truth might be in our time. The necessity for a "truth argument" arises precisely because it is in the realm of "truth arguments" that sensemaking occurs. People do not largely accept something that is a "rhetorical truth." "Rhetorical truth" is intended to mean that an argument in itself, a hermetic argument, may be logical but is self-referential. Such "rhetorical truth" cannot be on equal ground with something that people consider as important for their lives. And while it is no longer the case that we think of truth in a religious way, "truth arguments" nonetheless remain important for human beings in a very real and actual way.

A building unequivocally receives the fundamental legitimacy for its existence from its sense-making capabilities. In other words, the basic legitimacy of a building is a discourse on its sensemaking. However, the following must be stipulated as quickly as possible to avoid any misunderstanding: sense-making has nothing to do with a moral quest. There is no such thing as a moral or amoral building; there are only buildings that are sense-making or not. Sensemaking is not a question of goodness or badness; it is a question of right and wrong.

Authorship

Authorship creates sense-making buildings. Hence, authorship is also a reaction against the inability to design sense-making buildings in the non-referential world. It is the architect who works as the author—the "author-architect"—who is capable of conceiving such buildings in our non-referential world. It is highly unlikely that a team can accomplish something sense-making if authorship is not delegated to one of its architects. To design an ideational architecture that consists of rooms that can be experienced is a spiritual, speculative, and synthetic-creative act. This work is in the realm of the artistic-philosophical and not the organizational. A team without an author levels itself out and does not work metaphysically. However, because it has actively sought the ability to not believe in anything, our non-referential society does not have a basis and a canon anymore on which it can build in a sense-making way. With this in mind, a team consisting of various members can, at most, omit mistakes and create in a technical and organizationally scientific way but it is unable to create something sense-making. Yet, non-referential society demands an architecture that is sense-making by means of its presence and not one that explains. Sensemaking definitely requires the metaphysical which triggers speculation in the maker and the perceiver of architecture; and then makes the perceiver creative in their own right.

It is symptomatic that all of the most-admired architects in the past and present are a single person and not a team. A result of the postmodern ethical compass is to make believe that a group of mediocre people can become good if they work as a team. This belief has become a kind of ideologically driven and established "half-truth" in recent times. The destruction of the legitimacy of authorship of the autonomous architect is, as such, also an ideological act. The absolute desire to force into line and to level and homogenize everything has not only done away with the firmament above our heads and, moreover, seemingly successfully limited the magical, it also attempts to annihilate the ability to feel and empathize in a primordial, physical way. If that were ever to happen completely, it would end the discovery that lies at the heart of the aesthetic realm. However, it is in the nature of things for authorship to prevail.

It is under these current circumstances that the "author-architect" is important. The legitimacy of authors is, ultimately, timeless. The legitimacy is timeless because humankind ultimately supports the quest for sensemaking by individuals. It is an indelible fact about humankind that those who search for a "truth" have always existed. The "author-architect" is of that kind. Despite the scientization of our life, none of the fascination for "truth" has gone away. Such creativity for sensemaking in architecture—sense is not to be confused with purpose here—can only come from an author alone, because it is also the case that sense at its highest cannot ultimately be assessed.

In common parlance the author refers to the writer of a written work, but more broadly, an author is a person who gives existence to something new. The author takes responsibility for what they create and in doing this emphasizes the autonomous state of the author. A person who is autonomous acts independently. The model of the "author-architect" is a mentor and mastermind of a team with the propensity to be a creative thinker who has the artistic and intellectual capacity to build in the non-referential world.

The "author-architect" is not something new. Again, it is indicative that architects who have been admired throughout are so-called "author-architects." Despite the recent tenor of opinions claiming that individual architects are a role model of the past and are diminishing in importance, even today all architects who work creatively are "author-architects."

The actual need for "author-architects" has only become supremely paramount in recent times. Until the end of the era of postmodernism about twenty years ago, authorship in architecture was largely contained within the discipline of architecture, in the sense that it helped to move architecture within the ideational boundaries of a given epoch. Until the end of postmodernism, the architect was firmly embedded in the more or less fixed societal, philosophical, and professional aspiration of any given society and its culture. The architect's task was to build for those common societal values. This should not be understood as meaning that in the past even the best architects were building facilitators; it means that even the most admired and most provocative architects had the benefit of operating in the relative stability of more or less fixed sets of societal values. It was a source of comfort that architects could deduce larger societal currents for their own work. In lapidary terms, it may be stated that architects clearly knew what they had to do. The formidable task of the architect was to design beautiful and sense-making buildings as exemplifications of one or other world-conception. This task changed with the advent of the non-ref-erential world. Today, the task of the architect is to conceive buildings that are sense-making without having references to world-conceptions at hand. To confirm: "author-architects" are not only desir-able, they are unavoidable—without the work of "author-architects" it is not possible for our human quests to grow and to extend people's possibilities. What is different today is that the architect has no ideational apparatus that pre-defines what ought to be embodied in buildings. In fact, there is really nothing left to embody in the sense of a symbolic form that could be utilized. Yes, architects have always been form-givers of society to some extent. However, it is very difficult, if not impossible, to be a form-giver of a society that does not know its own form. Today, we can state that the task of architects is to modify expectations and to frame our lives. It is because of that societal shift towards the non-referential that architects must be authors for the most basic human quests. Instead of embodying something in a more or less symbolic way, the "author-architect" must conceive a basic framework in which people can think their thoughts. What "author-architects" are not, first: they are not makers of values in the sense of a megalomaniac establishment of values for other people. This is not possible because the "author-architect" of today does not know of any common values that possibly could be manifested in all or at least a great many buildings. What "author-architects" are not, second: there is the common misconception that the "author-architect" is dedicated foremost to their own self-realization and that the satisfaction of their own ego is in the foreground. The demand for "author-architects" is not about self-monumentalizing. Accordingly, just as their work is always public and never private, the "author-architect" is always a public figure. The "author-architect" does not practice self-discovery. The "author-architect" is not characterized by a turning into the self and by any kind of asocial reclusiveness. Instead, the "author-architect" alone is truly responsible towards society because they are dedicated to the discovery of that society's limits.

Contrary to the misconception that the "author-architect" works in isolation, the "author-architect" is the sleuth who seeks to establish how the world ticks. To be able to reflect on problems of this nature and scale, the architect has a keen understanding of the world. The architect has a flair for and access to the societal currents that move the world at a given time.

The "author-architect" offers buildings that add something new—in the common terminology of today, we could call it a "cultural added value"— that make people think, and thus bring movement to a society. That is the task! Everything else— functionality, construction, economic, and ecological concerns—is self-evident and the daily bread of designing and constructing buildings. These concerns are ultimately handiwork, craft, skills, organization, and the application of technological possibilities.

For example, the entire current discussion surrounding sustainability is a technical problem and perhaps also a political program, but it is surely not a quest for something sense-making and, as such, it is not interesting as a determining idea for a building. To avoid any misunderstanding here: this is not to argue that constructing buildings that are of the highest technical and constructive standards and perform well in relation to our environment is not a worthy cause. To reiterate, however, this is a technical issue.

One of the problems is that those who dedicate themselves almost exclusively to a particular technical issue in the design of a building attempt to elevate these singled-out concerns to a moral litmus test. In turn, sometimes such a singled-out concern even enters the realm of the political and becomes an even bigger litmus test there. However, such an approach is of no consequence for architecture and not generally valid for architecture. It must be expected that people will always have different moral convictions that are dependent on time, place, and history. Buildings cannot depend primarily on such fleeting foundations. This is one of the defining characteristics of an "author-architect," namely that an "author-architect" attempts to express something that is actual, as general as possible, and as close to truth—true in the sense of consequential—as possible. However, to stay with the aforementioned example, the realm of truth is neither economic nor un-economic, and it is neither ecological nor un-ecological. Instead, the sought for cultural added value stands squarely in the domain of sense-making.

The emphasis on sensemaking over technological issues and organization also addresses the question as to why, throughout history, the conceiving of consequential buildings originated entirely from the hands and minds of individual autonomous architects. Buildings can provide fundamental experiences of space in a spiritual, speculative, and synthetic-creative way, yet only the imagination of the single mind can create spaces that cause such experiences. A team of people, on the other hand, is not particularly well equipped to create such wonderment. A team composed of various members with diverse expertise is very well positioned and able to detect and omit mistakes. Furthermore, it can create technical and scientific solutions and it deals with organization exceedingly well, especially for large building projects. However, sense-making is not created by the minds of many but by the mind of one. The notion of the "collective mind" that is often attributed to a team is a figment and a misnomer. There is no such thing as a "collective mind." It does not exist. The mind, as such, is always bound to an individual human being. Sometimes a number of human beings work together, but ultimately the outcome of that team's work is not the sum total of all minds but only what the best one of these minds could ultimately imagine. In other words, the products of minds cannot simply be added in the creative-aesthetic domain.

To be clear: the "author-architect" does not work alone. Buildings always tend to be the work of a team in one way or another. The team contributes by finding technical solutions, detecting mistakes, and helping with the organization of designing, constructing, and erecting a building. However, no team substitutes for the presence of the "author-architect," who is the mastermind. The "author-architect" is also the person who makes decisions and bears responsibility. Most importantly, the "author-architect" has the capability to conceive the idea for a building and has an elevated taste that allows them to make judgments as to what is right and what is wrong.

The idea that the "author-architect" is an obsolete and old-fashioned model for the practice of architecture is a misconception encountered in too many areas within the field of architecture. It is madness to lead architects to believe that "author-architects" are a somehow reprehensible and culpable species. Such credos mostly stem from societal and political rationales and ideals that usually have little in common with judgments in the aesthetic domain and most often have nothing in common with the ability to design a building.

Just because the fact that more architects are less in command of their work does not justify the notion that "author-architects" are obsolete. On the contrary, "author-architects" are more important than ever today. However, architects as a whole are rendered of lesser importance precisely because there are fewer and fewer "author-architects." There are fewer "author-architects" because fewer architects can or want to be "author-architects." The primary reason for this decrease is not that architects are less talented or less capable than in the past, but that architects themselves do not have the confidence to want to be "author-architects" for reasons of societal pressure. It takes significant stamina and conviction for an architect to withstand the widespread suspicion about why a single person should have almost total authority over the construction of a building. The second reason why there are few "author-architects" is that others, such as marketing agents, clients, and city administrators, have stepped into the role to manage what is, in fact, the core of the architect's work. Increasingly, the expectation is that the role of the architect is a mere service provider, not unlike all the other involved parties in the manufacture of a building. As a result, it becomes a matter of the mere manufacture and not the fabrication of a building.

It is no exaggeration to state that without "author-architects" there will be no buildings that are sense-making. What we have without the work of "author-architects" are building as mere facilities. However, a building is only culturally and socially valuable, if there is also a speculative dimension—one could call it an idea, an intention, or a thesis that is sense-making. If there is no architect who conceives and designs sense-making buildings, buildings will be merely usable. However, a building's cultural and societal accomplishment is completed by means of an action by an architect that encompasses the realm of the intellectual, spiritual, speculative, and synthetic-creative. This is created through artistic and scientific innovation. Architects have a primordial task that they cannot give away. Architects cannot give away that task because there is simply nobody else who could meet this challenge. It is in the nature of the task that it is the architect who creates buildings that exist in the realm of the aesthetic and not solely in the realm of the utilitarian. When Vitruvius wrote that the task of architecture is to provide shelter, he did not mean that buildings solely provide a utilitarian roof over our heads. Instead, even if it has a big hole in it, or precisely because it has a big hole in it, a building's roof also shelters people metaphysically in the sense of the heavens' tent. These are the buildings that trigger repercussions in the souls and minds of people.

Valerio Olgiati, Markus Breitschmid
Non-Referential Architecture

Book design: Valerio Olgiati
Graphic Design: Bruno Margreth
Typesetting in RH Inter Pro Regular
Copy editing, Proofreading: Susan Cox,
Savannah Paige Murray, Louise Stein
Printing: Gulde Druck Tübingen
Paper: Munken Print White 1.5 100 gsm
Binding: Spinner Ottersweier

Park Books
Niederdorfstrasse 54, 8001 Zurich, Switzerland
www.park-books.com

Park Books is being supported by the Federal
Office of Culture with a general subsidy for
the years 2021–2024.

ISBN 978-3-03860-142-5